The
Social
Attitudes
of a
Catholic

Michael T. Ryan

Solidarity Books

Nihil obstat: Rev. Michael Smith
Imprimatur: Most Rev. R.P. Fabbro,
Bishop of London
March 7, 2005

ISBN 0-9737718-0-1

Library and Archives Canada Cataloguing in Publication

Ryan, Michael, 1926-

The social attitudes of a Catholic / Michael T. Ryan.

ISBN 0-9737718-0-1

1. Christian sociology--Catholic Church. 2. Church and social
problems--Catholic Church. I. Title.

BX2347.R92 2005   261.8'088'282   C2005-902054-7

Contents

Introduction

People sometimes speak about "turning their lives around." For a Christian this is an ongoing process. St. Paul tells us: "Your hearts and minds must be made completely new, and you must put on the new self, which is created in God's likeness and reveals itself in the true life which is upright and holy" *(Eph.* 4:23-24). His words are a call to *conversion.* We notice though that this conversion aims at becoming *completely* new. Putting on the new self means that *everything* about us must become converted, turned to God, and to others out of love for God.

When the bishops gathered in Rome for their 1971 Synod, to discuss justice in the world, they talked about some of the ways in which we fail to put on this new self, and so fall short of becoming the new man and woman of whom St. Paul speaks. They said, "The school and the communications media, which are often obstructed by the established order, allow the formation only of the man and woman desired by that order, that is to say, a man or woman in its own image, not a new man or woman, but a copy of man and woman as they are."

An American commentator on that statement made this frank comment: "The failure of American Catholic education is that it has made its students socially docile …. Far from being models the rest of us can look up to, they bear a distressing resemblance to everyone else."

A good deal of the time, this failure is not due simply to a lack of good will. The problem arises from the fact that conversion calls for both a change of heart and a change in attitudes. Nowhere is this more obvious than in the case of our *social attitudes*. One of the great truths illuminated by 20th century philosophy is the crucial importance of our attitudes, that is, the role played by the ways in which we look at, or picture, the world around us.

Paul Ricoeur writes: "Every real conversion is first a revolution on the level of our directive images. By changing his imagination, a man changes his existence." Ludwig Wittgenstein, who so marvellously illustrated the many different ways in which words function, pointed out that our philosophical "problems" often arise from the fact that "a picture holds us captive"; our problem is the mental image we tend to associate with a particular word.

In a wonderful little book dealing with being a Catholic in the modern world, the theologian, Romano Guardini, insists that many of the difficulties Christians experience with belief today result not from a failure of faith but from a failure of imagination; they are associating some truth of faith with a faulty picture. After all, St. Thomas Aquinas makes it clear that, because our knowledge, and so our language, depends on sense experience, we always associate an idea with some picture or image in our imagination. Those images, pictures, or attitudes, often need change or conversion. That is why I have entitled the following short articles on Catholic social teaching, "the *social attitudes* of a Catholic." They have to do primarily with the mental pictures or images we associate with various social realities.

Needless to say, these articles deal only with *some* social justice issues. Moreover, since Catholic social teaching has traditionally been regarded as dealing primarily with economic questions there are no articles on abortion or other bioethical matters, on which, in any case, abundant literature is available.

I thank the people who read and commented on most of these articles in an earlier draft, especially Father Michael Smith, Father Leonard Kennedy, C.S.B., and Father Richard Charrette. I also owe a debt of gratitude to Mr. Ron Pickersgill for his generous help in preparing this material for publication and for handling the many technical details involved in printing the book.

Discussion groups

This text is designed primarily for use by discussion groups. Each article is followed by a list of resources and several questions. A group will need a capable and dedicated leader, and group members should commit themselves to active participation. The group should decide how many articles it wants to deal with each week. For example, a group might discuss three articles a week for ten weeks, or four articles a week for seven weeks. Group members need to read the assigned articles during the week before their meeting, and write down their answers to the questions attached to each article.

The following format is suggested for the weekly meeting itself:

- The meeting should open with prayer, perhaps something recited together.

- The group leader or someone appointed by the leader then follows with a prayerful reading of one of the suggested biblical texts. This is followed by a reflective reading of one of the corresponding texts from Catholic social documents.

- The leader then guides the meeting through the assigned chapters by reading out the individual questions for each chapter and asking the group members how they answered the question in each case. As members compare their answers the way is opened up for some fruitful discussion, especially if the leader gently keeps people on topic.

- The evening might end with the viewing of one of the suggested videos for the material being considered at that meeting.

Ideally, the meeting would last an hour and a half, but should go no longer than two hours in any case.

Where to find the Church's social documents

The texts of most of the social documents of the Catholic Church can be found on a website known as *The Catholic Labour Network*. Go to www. catholiclabor.org and click on "Papal encyclicals".

There is also a collection of the Church's social documents in print. It is entitled *Catholic Social Thought: The Documentary Heritage,* edited by David O'Brien and Thomas Shannon. It is available from Orbis Books.

There are also many good commentaries on Catholic social teaching. In particular, we are fortunate to have available now the *Compendium of the Social Doctrine of the Church*, an official Vatican publication. It is available from the Publications Office of the Canadian Conference of Catholic Bishops (www.cccbpublications.net).

1. Christian morality: personal or social?

In the 1970s, after the major Canadian Christian churches had cooperated in establishing several ecumenical coalitions to address various justice issues, an Ontario Catholic educator wrote a critical article. Churches, he wrote, were no longer places of peace: "I say the time has come to get the churches out of politics and politics out of the churches." Meanwhile in England, the respected scholar Edward Norman wrote: "A reading of the Gospels less indebted to present values will reveal the true Christ of history in the spiritual depiction of a man who directed others to turn away from the preoccupations of human society …. In the Gospels, the teachings of the Saviour clearly describe a personal rather than a social morality." (*Christianity and Social Order*, Oxford 1979, pp. 78-80).

These people reflect an individualist approach to the Gospels; they see Christian morality as concerned mostly with the conversion of the individual.

About the same time, George Pixley, a Protestant seminary professor in Mexico City, saw things differently. Reflecting on the social impact of fundamentalist preachers in Latin American countries, he said: "They believe that social problems can be cured through improving oneself. We believe that the deep problems in Latin American society can be solved only if people organize and make structural changes. But the sects effectively undercut any political participation outside the church, like union activities. They demobilize people." (Marlise Simons, "Latin America's New Gospel," *The New York Times Magazine*, Nov. 7, 1982).

The struggle between those who see Christianity as preaching a "purely personal" morality and those who believe the gospel has clear social implications continues today. When the Canadian bishops issued their 1983 statement on the economic crisis, several politicians, including some Catholics, accused the Church of stepping outside its proper sphere and interfering in politics. More recently, others have insisted that the Church should confine itself to "spiritual" matters and leave "financial" issues to others. Such challenges ignore an astounding official movement that has grown and matured in the Catholic Church for more than a century.

In 1891, Pope Pope Leo XIII published the first official, authoritative statement reflecting the conviction that following Jesus Christ involves not only issues of personal morality but also social attitudes and positions. That document was followed by ten others. The documents are, in order of appearance:

- Pope Leo XIII, *Rerum Novarum (The Condition of the Working Classes)* 1891

- Pope Pius XI, *Quadragesimo Anno (Reconstructing the Social Order)* 1931

- Pope John XXIII, *Mater et Magistra (Mother and Teacher)* 1961

- Pope John XXIII, *Pacem in Terris (Peace on Earth)* 1963

- Vatican II, *Gaudium et Spes (The Church in the Modern World)* 1965

- Pope Paul VI, *Populorum Progressio (The Development of Peoples)* 1967

- Pope Paul VI, *Octogesima Adveniens (The Eightieth Anniversary)* 1971

- Second Synod of Bishops, *Justice in the World*, 1971

- Pope John Paul II, *Laborem Exercens (On Human Work)* 1981

- Pope John Paul II, *Sollicitudo Rei Socialis (Social Concern of the Church)* 1987

- Pope John Paul II, *Centesimus Annus (The Hundredth Anniversary)* 1991

There is a remarkable development in their teaching over those one hundred years. While *Rerum Novarum* is mostly a protest against certain injustices in industrialized countries, *Quadragesimo Anno* has positive proposals for a just reconstruction of the entire social order. *Mater et Magistra* and *Pacem in Terris* go beyond industrialized countries and look to what is needed, both to root out injustices and to create a more human life for people all over the world. *Gaudium et Spes* portrays a whole new attitude that the Christian should take toward our present world and toward relations with all people of good will. *Populorum Progressio, Octogesima Adveniens* and *Sollicitudo Rei Socialis* develop a vision of a world where all people are able to participate in the movements that shape their life and can live with dignity. *Laborem Exercens* develops a rich theology of human work, showing how being created "in the image of God" means each person has a right to perform worthwhile work and so share in the care of this world. *Centesimus Annus* offers a vision of what it means to be a genuine "economic person."

This body of Catholic social teaching reflects the Church's conviction, *first,* that there is a social message in the gospels; *second,* that it is the Church's role, guided by the Holy Spirit, to unfold and make explicit that message; *third,* that new cultural conditions often enable us to see more clearly aspects of the gospel that were not as apparent to earlier ages. It is appropriate then to see Catholic social teaching as an instance of a legitimate "development of doctrine."

How should these documents of Catholic social teaching be read?

With faith. They are expressions of the ordinary magisterium of the Church, to which a faithful Catholic owes "internal and religious assent." Though they are not infallible documents, we need to keep in mind the words of Pope John XXIII: "We firmly assert that the social doctrine professed by the Catholic Church is a necessary part of its teaching on how people should live." (*Mater et Magistra*, no. 222).

With awareness of the cultural elements they contain. Just as God the Son took on a particular human nature, becoming a Jewish man in a particular time and place, so these documents contain elements that reflect the culture of the time they were written. Such cultural elements need to be distinguished from the basic message.

With a sense of history. We need to read each document in context. What events and concerns shaped that particular time in which it was written? We must also relate each document to both earlier and later documents. As we compare the various documents, we are aware of development, growth, and, occasionally, a reversal of positions previously held. So we need to beware of engaging in "encyclical fundamentalism." What *Quadragesimo Anno* meant by "socialism", for example, is quite different from what *Laborem Exercens* means by it.

With care. A great deal of preparation and consultation went into these documents. They demand careful and respectful reading. This is much more the case in more recent social documents, since they come from a church that is more conscious of its right and duty to speak out on social issues, and that consults widely in the preparation of its social statements.

1. Christian morality: personal or social?

Resources for Discussion:

Scripture: *Isaiah* 58: 6-8

Social Documents: *Rerum Novarum*, no. 2; *Quadragesimo Anno*, no. 135. *Mater et Magistra*, nos. 222-225; *Centesimus Annus*, no. 43.

Questions for Discussion:

- How much awareness do you think most Catholics have of the Church's social teaching?

- Most bishops and priests have no special qualifications in economics or politics. Shouldn't the Church, therefore, leave economics and politics to the economists and politicians?

- Some years ago, a prominent lay leader in the United States said: "As American Catholics have made it into the mainstream, they, like American Protestants, have privatized their faith." Do you think this is also the case in Canada?

- Do you think the sex abuse scandals stand in the way of people paying attention to the social pronouncements of the Church? If so, what can we do about it?

Suggested video resource to end the meeting

Bring Down the Walls (United States Catholic Conference)

2. Spirituality or justice?

When I was a young priest in the mid-1950s, I was stationed in a parish that was responsible for a community hospital. I was in and out of that hospital a great deal. The administrator's office was near the front door, and often he would greet me with the words, "Are you saving lots of souls?" That question used to irritate me. Yet there was some basis for it in the common outlook of the day. After all, we Catholics would often say that the one thing that mattered was *to save your soul*. This present world was seen as a danger to that, and so at the end of each Mass we used to pray that we would be safely conducted through "this valley of tears."

The Second Vatican Council presented Catholics with a different way of looking at this world. Instead of regarding our present world as a "valley of tears", we were encouraged to care for this present world. The *Constitution on the Church in the Modern World* begins with the words: "The joys and the hopes, the griefs and the anxieties of the people of this age … these are the joys and hopes, the griefs and anxieties of the followers of Christ." The document goes on: "While we are warned that it profits persons nothing if they gain the whole world, yet lose themselves, the expectation of a new earth must not weaken but rather stimulate our concern for cultivating this one" (no. 39).

This raises a question for us. Where should our efforts be directed: toward getting to *the next world*, or toward making *this world* a better place? In some parts of the Catholic world this contrast is very visible today. For example, in some parts of Latin America there are bishops, priests, and laity who are in movements preoccupied with individual spirituality. Their emphasis is on a personal prayer experience. Other bishops, priests, and lay people are devoted to movements concerned with social transformation. Their emphasis is on applying the gospel to this world in order to change it.

So, what is being a Christian all about? Is it about getting to heaven or is it about improving this world? Is it about spirituality or is it about justice?

Clearly, it is about *both* and, indeed, *both together*. We can't improve this world if we aren't trying to get to heaven, and we can't get to heaven if we aren't trying to improve this world. The great 20th century apostle of the poor in the United States, Dorothy Day, whose cause for canonization is under way, writes:

"The greatest challenge of the day is how to bring about a revolution of the heart, a revolution that has to start with each one of us. When we begin to take the lowest place, to wash the feet of others, to love our brothers and sisters with that burning love, that passion, which led to the Cross, then we can truly say 'Now I have begun'."

Without this *personal conversion*, this *conversion of the heart,* which involves a life of prayer, we can do nothing that counts as genuine Christian action. At the same time, the bishops gathered in Rome for their 1971 Synod, declared: "Action for the sake of justice and participation in the transformation of the world fully appear to us to be a constitutive element of the preaching of the gospel."

Much depends on our *image* of the Church. The Church is not just a community to give us personal peace, a place to which we can retreat from the burdens and troubles of life to be soothed and calmed. The last thing we want, if this is how we view the Church, is a sermon that talks about politics, or a liturgy that interferes with our personal conversation with God. This very private view of the Church is opposed to the teaching of the *Constitution on the Church in the Modern World*, that we can no longer be content with "a merely individualistic morality" (no. 30). Dorothy Day writes, "To be in church isn't to be calmed down. I'm worked up in church."

Nor is the Church a kind of community to ensure social peace, a spiritual policeman, standing shoulder to shoulder with the government as a defender of the *status quo*. This image is a constant temptation for the Church, and there have been times when Church leaders have accepted it, sometimes with disastrous results for the Church's mission.

Rather, the Church is a community engaged in bringing about change, as Pope Paul VI pictures it in his 1975 document on evangelization. It is *the yeast of the gospel*, and as such is here to bring about necessary changes in everything — human persons, cultures, social structures, public relationships — everything! This also means that conversion must be both personal and social; it must affect both our heart and our attitudes.

The Reverend Jesse Jackson once remarked, "When I pray 'Thy Kingdom come', I mean that Atlanta should look like heaven." There is no genuine prayer that does not concern itself with the common good. At the same time, the very first thing each of us must do for the common good is pray for our own personal conversion.

Resources for Discussion:

Scripture: *Jeremiah* 29: 4-7

Social Documents: *Constitution on the Church in the Modern World*, nos. 1 and 2

Questions for Discussion:

- Of the three images of the Church presented, which one has been most prevalent in your life?

- Has the Church been placed here in the world for the sake of the Church or for the sake of the world?

Suggested video to end the meeting:

Committed to Change (Canadian Catholic Organization for Development and Peace)

3. Our culture: friend or enemy?

On a warm summer day in Toronto I was fascinated by the sight of several Muslim women, clothed from head to toe in black robes, mingling with people in brief attire, on the ferry to Centre Island. The contrast they presented between religion and culture was startling. Yet there is nothing new about such contrasts. In 1949, the Yale theologian, H. Richard Niebuhr, delivered a famous set of lectures entitled *Christ and Culture*. What is the relationship between our faith and our culture? To be a Christian means to commit our entire self, in every way, to Christ. To be a member of 21st century Canadian society means to accommodate our lives to the world in which we live. Can we do both? Or is our culture the enemy of our faith, something we have to oppose if we are going to be faithful to the gospel? The effort to answer that question brings us to the very heart of Catholic social teaching.

When Pope Leo XIII published the first Catholic social document, *Rerum Novarum* ("The New Things") in 1891, one of its most startling features was its positive approach to the culture of its day. For a good part of the 19th century, the church had distanced itself from the economic and civic developments taking place. By contrast, Pope Leo insisted that this world is not our enemy. Instead of condemning all that was modern ("the new things"), he accepted the world he found and showed how to work with it to protect and advance the dignity of people.

That new spirit found some of its greatest expressions in the social documents of Pope John XXIII and Second Vatican Council. These documents speak of "caring for the world", and of looking for the "signs of the Spirit" in our world.

What perhaps was new for many Catholics in all this was the assertion that God is at work in the world, and not just in the Church. The hand of God could be detected in some "secular" movements, such as initiatives for peace, efforts to recognize the rights of minorities, and expressions of concern for the protection of the environment. Catholics should therefore work with such "secular" efforts and try to assist them.

"With the help of the Holy Spirit, it is the task of the entire People of God, especially pastors and theologians, to hear, distinguish and interpret *the many voices of our age*, and to judge them in the light of the divine Word, so that revealed truth can always be more deeply penetrated, better understood and set forth to greater advantage." *(Constitution on the Church in the Modern World,* no. 44. Italics added)

At the same time, Catholic social documents call our attention to major currents in our world and our culture that are *opposed* to the gospel. As followers of Christ, we must reject such currents. Pope Paul VI wrote, "the split between the gospel and culture is without a doubt the tragedy of our time" (*Evangelization in the Modern World,* no. 20).

Four of the more influential features of our culture from which Catholics should distance ourselves, are the following.

Individualism – Our society glamourizes "the rugged individual", and praises aggressiveness. It is a spirit that is evident in everything from cut-throat business practices to selfish driving habits. In contrast, Christians should remind society that there is no such thing as a "pure individual. " Humans are *persons*, and persons are inherently *social*. To be "you" means to be part of a family, part of a particular ethnic group, part of a civic community, and so on. These groups "define" us, make us, in many ways, *who* we are. At the same time, we have responsibilities to all of them, and in turn we give a shape to them. (Note how the "myth of the individual" is deliberately used today to promote the view that religion is a purely private matter with no place in the public forum. In fact our faith has social consequences, and so is bound to contribute to the shape of our culture.)

Materialism – One of the most harmful lies our culture has continued to tell us since the 17th century is that humans find their fulfillment in *possession.* Newspapers and television ads, for example, urge us constantly to "consume," to "purchase," Yet we are not just consumers. We are human beings who find our fulfillment in "using" the goods of this earth as *means* to intelligent goals. What matters in life is to pursue worthwhile goals, to carry out roles that make our world and society somehow better.

Relativism – It is common to have people ask "Is it true *for you*?" or "Is it right *for you*?" Yet guides for conduct cannot be true for one person and not true for another. What we have in common is our humanity. What develops or perfects that humanity is dictated by our common nature, not by what we "feel" like doing. Truth is something *objective.* "Facts," it is said, "are stubborn things." You can't ignore them.

Secularism – Reflecting on the terrible attacks on human life in our world, from genocide to wars of aggression and terrorism, from abortion to euthanasia, from arbitrary imprisonment to disgraceful working conditions, Pope John Paul II sought the roots of the struggle between "the culture of life" and the "culture of death". He concluded: "We have to go to the heart of the tragedy being experienced by modern man: the eclipse of the sense of God and of man, typical of a social and cultural climate dominated by *secularism.*" (*The Gospel of Life,* no. 21. Italics added) "When the sense of God is lost, the sense of man is also threatened and poisoned." (no. 22)

(Sadly religion is also sometimes *misused* to justify actions that work *against* human life.)

What needs especially to concern us about these trends in our culture is that they are not just faults of individuals. They are features of many of our social and economic structures. As such, they surround us, envelop us, and seduce us.

So, Christ or culture? It is a matter of careful discernment. We need to love our world; we must recognize and affirm whatever is true and good in it, looking especially for signs of God's action in our culture. Much of Catholic social teaching deals with ways in which we can do this. We also need to oppose the trends in our culture that work against true human dignity. In this respect Catholic social teaching calls on us to be a highly visible "contrast society."

Resources for Discussion:

Scripture: *I Peter* 2: 11-17

Social Documents: *Constitution on the Church in the Modern World*, nos. 57-59

Questions for Discussion:

- What criteria should we employ to determine if a particular feature of our culture, or "sign of our time," is actually a sign of the Spirit?

- Using those criteria, where is God at work in present-day secular movements?

- Besides those already listed, what other features of our culture do you believe we should denounce and oppose?

- What are some of the ways in which individualism manifests itself in our society?

Suggested video to end the meeting:

Manufacturing Consent: Noam Chomsky and the Media (National Film Board of Canada) selected passages.

4. What do we mean by "the dignity of the human person"?

Imagine a priest who opened his Sunday homily with the words: "Dear Sunday collection contributors." People would be offended, and with good reason, for that would be a *reductive* form of address. Persons are much more than Sunday collection contributors! Yet there is another reductive expression that our society uses all the time. It refers to us as "consumers". Consider how offensive that is. Cats and dogs and horses and cows are consumers. They consume, and are in turn consumed themselves, because they are simply part of nature. Humans however are not just part of nature. In one important respect, humans rise above nature, for God has made humans the *stewards* or *managers* of nature. This basic insight appears in the very first book of the Bible: "Let us make humankind in our image, according to our likeness, and let them have dominion over the fish of the sea, and over the birds of the air, and over the cattle, and over all the wild animals of the earth, and over every creeping thing that creeps upon the earth" (*Genesis* 1:26).

If you read the writings of Pope John Paul II carefully, you will notice how often he refers to humans as *subjects*. Human persons are the only creatures on this earth that are subjects. Dogs and cats, for example, are not subjects. A subject is someone who is *self-directed*, and so is capable of assuming responsibility for himself or herself, as well as for other things. When *Genesis* speaks of human persons as made in God's image and likeness, it means that God has made humans capable of assuming responsibility, like God. God did that because God intends human persons to serve as God's managers in caring for God's world and for human society. This special dignity that God bestowed on humans was then raised to a new and greater level when God the Son took on a human nature and lived as one of us.

One consequence of the fact that humans have dignity is that, since persons are "subjects," it is always wrong to treat them simply as "objects." Social practices or customs that reduce persons to purely passive roles, in the workplace, in politics, in the life of the Church, are wrong, because such practices and customs treat person as objects. Adam Smith, the father of modern economics, reduced persons to objects when he said, "The worker is only an instrument purchased by the employer for a certain task." Pope Leo XIII protested against such views when he stated that human work is not a commodity. One of the reasons why the Church defends the right of workers to form labour unions, is that it sees in paternalism an attitude that is offensive to human dignity. The employer who says, "You don't need a union; I will take care of you," is failing to recognize the importance of human persons speaking and acting for themselves, as responsible subjects.

A second consequence of human dignity is the fact that only human beings have *rights*. Animals do not have "rights." As managers for God, human persons have a strict obligation to treat animals with respect for their place in nature, remembering always that they are God's creatures, and not subjecting them to unnecessary suffering. At the same time we must not lose sight of the unique status of human persons. Some environmentalists suggest that humans are just one more species in nature, on equal terms with all other species. This is incorrect. Humans have dignity. This gives us a special status in nature, but it also brings with it a great responsibility toward nature, to manage all of it according to God's laws (and so according to nature's laws).

A third consequence of human dignity can be gathered from the very meaning of the word. A "dignity" is something that stands on its own, something that is not just a means to something else. In Aristotle's logic, for example, a "dignity" is a first principle. Humans have dignity because their purpose in life, to know, love, and serve God, stands on its own. It coincides with the purpose of creation. The human being is the "only creature on earth which God willed for itself", says Vatican II's *Constitution on the Church in the Modern World* (no. 24). Ultimately, human persons have dignity because we alone, on this earth, are able to know God, and so are able to respond to

4. What do we mean by "the dignity of the human person"?

God, in the name of everything else on earth. The biblical passage, "All you winds, bless the Lord, fire and heat, bless the Lord, cold and chill, bless the Lord," means that it is our great vocation to bless the Lord on behalf of all these natural realities that are incapable of knowing God themselves. Our dignity as human persons is never more evident than when we are on our knees, praising the God who created and sustains all that we see.

Resources for Discussion:

Scripture: *Psalm 8*

Social Documents: *Mater et Magistra*, nos. 218-221; *Pacem in Terris*, nos. 9-10; *Laborem Exercens*, no. 6

Questions for Discussion:

- Do you find it offensive to be addressed as a "consumer"?

- Can you think of situations that treat persons as "objects"?

- What is your assessment of "animal rights" groups you know or have heard about?

5. Individuals or social beings?

Margaret Thatcher, the "Iron Lady" who was prime minister of Britain in the 1980s, was one of the principal architects of the political conservatism that has become common in some western democracies. She once made the astounding statement, "There is no such thing as society. There are only individuals." It is often pointed out that *individualism* is a prominent characteristic of our culture. But the practice of regarding persons as "individuals" began around the 17th century. That was when supporters of the new market economy began to portray people as "isolated individuals," competing with one another in pursuit of their selfish private interests.

In contrast, it makes more sense to assert that there is no such thing as a pure individual. What exist are *human persons*, and persons are profoundly *social*. We exist and have our identities only as members of various communities. To be *you* is to be part of a particular family, member of a particular ethnic community, citizen of a particular country, formed by a particular culture. These various communities make us the persons we are. Each of us has our place within them, and we have responsibilities as members of them. Catholic social teaching reflects this communal character we all possess in two principles.

The *principle of solidarity* asserts that society is something like a *family*. Canada, for example, is not just a collection of 31 million individuals. We have a life together, in which we are pursuing common ends by common means. We are interdependent. One of the consequences of this principle is that there are certain things all of us should be able to count on simply because we are part of the family. This is why we have universal social programs. People who reach the age of sixty-five, for example, are entitled to the old age pension, whether they are rich or poor. It is our family's way of recognizing the role they have played in building up our country over the years. Persons who are sick are entitled to proper medical care, whether they have money or not. It is our family's way of acknowledging that every person has dignity. We call such programs *universal* to indicate that they do not "single out", "target" or "stigmatize" certain people or groups of people, but treat all of us the same. The principle of solidarity also demands that we should not institute economic measures that callously sacrifice certain members of the family, like monetary policies that deliberately cause unemployment.

The *principle of subsidiarity* asserts that society is something like *a human body*. This ancient comparison is used to make the point that a healthy society, like the human body, has different organs to perform different functions on behalf of the entire body. We have ears that hear for the good of the whole body, feet that walk for the good of the entire body, and so on.

Similarly, a good society has, within it, many smaller societies through which the life of that society is carried on. We have families to raise children, professional groups to set standards for the services we need, labour unions to represent particular groups of workers, political parties to offer visions for government, agricultural bodies to serve as the voice of farmers, and so on.

It is a violation of subsidiarity if the state stands in the way of such "intermediate societies", or if it takes over from them functions that they are able to carry out themselves. Parents, for example, even have the right to "home school" their children, as long as they prepare them adequately for higher education.

Subsidarity is an important principle, because normally it is through "smaller" or "lower" groups that persons have input into social life, and can make their voice heard in the larger society. This principle is widely ignored today, with disastrous results. The anti-globalization movement is a protest, not so much against "bigness" as against an organization of our economy that does not allow ordinary people to have input into the decisions that affect their lives. Many would argue also that some provincial government policies in Ontario have violated the principle of subsidiarity. The creation of larger school boards, along with the removal of their power to tax, takes away or reduces the opportunity for people to have genuine input into decisions affecting their own local schools. Some would use a similar argument to oppose the creation of "megacities." Moves of this kind are usually defended in the name of "efficiency." One may well question however if they are really efficient in helping to create a more human society. That, after all, is the goal that matters most to all of us.

Resources for Discussion:

Scripture: *Acts* 2: 43-47

Social Documents: *Quadragesimo Anno*, nos. 79-80; *Pacem in Terris,* nos. 23-24; *Sollicitudo Rei Socialis*, no. 39

Questions for Discussion:

- What are some of the ways in which you can see that you are a social being?

- What are some examples of government programs that "target" certain people? Can you think of a way to change such programs?

- In what ways do you see the principle of subsidiarity being violated in our society?

6. What is "the common good"?

The Quebec Summit of 2001 gave Canadians a front row seat for the free trade debate. Leaders of 34 countries in the Americas met in Quebec City to promote expanded free trade, while a few days earlier the People's Summit met to oppose the proposed expansion. There were also several public demonstrations opposed to greater free trade during the Quebec City meeting. Expanded free trade is clearly an issue on which people have strong, opposing convictions. What are we to think of this debate? Can Catholic social teaching provide us any guidance? Clearly, there is no simple answer to such a complex issue. However one way of viewing this debate is to see it as a battle between conflicting views of what is meant by "the common good."

The common good is a centuries-old notion in Catholic teaching. It is also a notion that has been prominent in recent Catholic social documents. For example, the Catholic Bishops of England and Wales entitled their 1996 guide for Christian political action, *The Common Good*.

Yet what is the "common good"? Briefly, it is the good that we receive as members of some social group, and moreover, a good that we can get *only* by being members of that group. It is truly a good that each of us receives, it is a *personal* good, but it is one we get only by doing our part as members of some group.

The common good of a baseball team is winning ball games. We share in that good only by being active members of that team. The common good of a monastery or convent is the atmosphere of faith and love that the members create together, and which they all share. The common good of a neighbourhood is the safe and healthy social climate that the people living there bring about by their joint action, for example, through initiatives like "Neighbourhood Watch." Usually, the common good has a spiritual quality.

The common good of any group or society can exist only if there are laws and social arrangements to promote it, and if the members of that society are prepared to sacrifice some of their private wants in order to maintain that good. A baseball player, for example, must be prepared to play the position where he or she can best serve the team, not the position he or she personally prefers. A member of a religious community must sacrifice private activities in order to be present for community prayers and gatherings.

In recent times, a false view of "the common good" has become popular. This is the view that the common good consists in the removal of as many obstacles as possible to private activity. In this view, there is really no *common* good that is pursued at all. There is simply a public domain, protected by law, in which each person or enterprise is free to pursue their *private* good, with as little social or legal restraint as possible. No talk here of sacrificing our private wants, or making our contribution, so that together we may all enjoy a good that we could never obtain by ourselves alone. There is only talk of creating a public space for private gain.

The "free trade" debate reflects, in some ways, a contest between these two views of the common good. Many proponents of free trade, for example, argue for the elimination of all "barriers" to economic activity, such as labour standards and environmental safeguards. One wonders what kind of common good is being created as a result.

The Second Vatican Council worried about the rise of a spirit of "economism". "Many people, especially in economically advanced areas, seem, as it were, to be ruled by economics, so that almost their entire personal and social life is permeated with a certain economic way of thinking" (*Constitution on the Church in the Modern World,* no. 63).

We need to trade as nations. We need to remove *unnecessary* obstacles to economic activity. But the common good requires that we put in place the kind of legal framework that will safeguard, and *actively promote*, respect for all human rights, both civil-political and socio-economic, decent living standards, just wages and working conditions, and genuine care of our world.

6. What is "the common good"?

Only in this way can we hope to bring about, through our joint activity as nations, an international community in which all of us will share in a better, more fully human, life than any of our countries could have provided for us simply by acting alone.

Resources for Discussion:

Scripture: *Ephesians* 4: 1-16.

Social Documents: *Constitution on the Church in the Modern World*, no. 75

Questions for Discussion:

- There are many "common goods" just as there are many different social groups. Can you identify the common good of a family? Of a school classroom? Of a parish?

- What do you think has been the impact of the North American Free Trade Agreement on the common good in Canada?

- What are some of the ways in which our country's trading policies could be changed in order to promote more effectively the *global* common good?

Suggested video to end the meeting:

The Emperor's New Clothes (National Film Board of Canada)

7. Human rights

"It's my right!" This is a claim often heard today; it is at the root of many lawsuits. While all of us are thankful to be living in a country where human rights are usually respected, we may also feel at times, when we look at what some people are claiming as their right, that there is some confusion in the public mind as to what genuinely is a human right, and what is not.

The language of human rights has a secular origin in the French Revolution and the Enlightenment. A major landmark in this secular movement to promote human rights occurred in the 20th century when the United Nations adopted the Universal Declaration of Human Rights on December 10, 1948. That declaration served as a model that individual countries were encouraged to follow. In our own country the Canadian Charter of Rights and Freedoms became law on April 17, 1982. We owe a debt of gratitude to the pioneers in the secular human rights movement.

As Robert Soler has demonstrated however, the actual *substance* of human rights talk goes back to the 16th century and to a movement that involved leading Catholic thinkers as well as Pope Paul III. Catholic writers like Bartolomé de las Casas and Francisco de Vitoria defended the human rights of the Indian population in Central and South America and so laid the groundwork for much present-day work in human rights ("A Catholic Perspective on Human Rights", *The Tablet,* July 26/03, p. 14).

The Catholic Church has issued its own declaration of human rights. On April 11, 1963, Pope John XXIII published *Pacem in Terris* (Peace on Earth), which defended human rights at all levels, individual, national and international. Robert Hutchins, former President of the University of Chicago, described this encyclical as "one of the most profound and significant documents of our age." Its treatment of human rights contrasts in important ways with the way rights are commonly understood by secular society.

7. Human rights

First, the secular movement to defend and promote human rights developed in a largely *non-religious* atmosphere (although there were a number of believers among the early human rights theorists). So, it is somewhat vague on *why* human beings have rights. Consequently, there is a temptation to view human rights in a self-centered way. A right tends to be regarded as what I require for my self-expression.

The Catholic defence of human rights, by contrast, sees rights as what are required by human dignity, and views that dignity as rooted in God. Humans have dignity because they are capable of knowing and loving God. Hence, in the Catholic tradition, genuine human rights always have a spiritual character. They concern what we are entitled to in order to become what God intended us to be.

Second, the secular human rights movement tends to view humans in an individualistic way. Catholic teaching, however, insists that humans are naturally *social*, and have responsibilities or duties that arise from their roles in the various societies of which they are part. This is why Catholic social thought speaks of a human right as a moral capacity to do what I have a responsibility or duty to do, a duty either to God or to some human community. I have a duty to carry out my role as an image of God in caring for God's world; hence I have a natural right to gainful employment. I have a duty to care for my family; hence I have a natural right to a living wage.

Third, it is clear, in the Catholic tradition, that there is a fundamental difference between a genuine human right and a mere individual advantage. I have a human right to practise my religion, or to know the truth, but I do not have a human right to make a million dollars or to get drunk. Think of it as follows. Most people recognize that our human rights are limited by the rights of others; for example, my right to free movement is limited by your right to privacy. However human rights are also limited by the very nature of a right. I have a natural right to what I truly need in order to carry out my responsibilities, but I do not have a natural right to whatever my heart happens to desire.

We need to be vigourous in our defence and promotion of human rights. Yet we also need to be quite clear on what is truly a human right and what is not.

Resources for Discussion:

Scripture: *Romans* 2: 14-16

Social Documents: *Pacem in Terris*, nos. 142-145

Questions for Discussion:

- Identify some of the things often referred to as "rights" in our society that in fact have no moral foundation as human rights.

- What genuine human rights do you see that our society fails to protect?

8. Charity or justice: social service or social action?

A few years ago the following story appeared in the *Review for Religious*. "Once there was a farming town that could be reached by a narrow road with a bad curve in it. There were frequent accidents on the road especially at the curve, and the preacher would preach to the people of the town to make sure they were Good Samaritans. And so they were, as they would pick up the people on the road, for this was a religious work. One day someone suggested they buy an ambulance to get accident victims to the town hospital more quickly. The preacher preached and the people gave, for this was a religious work. Then one day a councilman suggested that the town authorize building a wider road and taking out the dangerous curve. Now it happened that the mayor had a farm market right at the curve on the road and he was against taking out the curve. Someone asked the preacher to say a word to the mayor and the congregation next Sunday about it. But the preacher and most of the people figured they had better stay out of politics; so next Sunday the preacher preached on the Good Samaritan Gospel and encouraged the people to continue their fine work of picking up the accident victims – which they did." The story brings out very well the difference between justice and some of the things we usually call "charity."

In their book, *The Church and Social Justice*, Calvez and Perrin describe three meanings of the word "charity" in the Church's social documents. First, "charity" sometimes means the *works* of charity, or what we might call "social service" as distinguished from "social action." The social encyclicals often praise the works of charity practised by Christians throughout the centuries. Pope Leo XIII reminds us of the tradition going all the way back to the *Acts of the Apostles* of feeding the hungry and caring for the poor. He speaks of religious communities founded to look after orphans, care for the sick, and give refuge to the elderly. Pope John Paul makes the same point in *Centesimus Annus,* number 49. This is a noble tradition and we could not envisage the Christian life without it.

Second, "charity" sometimes refers to actions that have become a *substitute* for justice. Pope Pius XI makes the famous statement in *Quadragesimo Anno* that "Charity cannot take the place of justice unfairly withheld." (no. 137). Earlier in the same document, referring to the terrible poverty accompanying the industrial revolution, he says: "This state of things was quite satisfactory to the wealthy, who looked upon it as the consequence of inevitable economic laws, and who therefore were content to leave to charity alone the full care of helping the unfortunate; as though it were the task of charity to make amends for the open violation of justice, a violation not merely tolerated, but sometimes even ratified, by legislators." (no. 4). It is very important to take note of this meaning of charity as a "substitute for justice", because this is a constant temptation for all of us.

Third, "charity" refers most appropriately to the Christian *virtue* of charity which is essential to the Christian life. In this connection St. Thomas Aquinas reminds us that "Charity is the form of all the virtues," in the sense that no action can possibly be described as virtuous unless it proceeds from charity, that is from love of God and love of our neighbour for the love of God (cf. *Matt.* 22:40). Justice that is not motivated by charity is not justice at all, and can result in seriously misguided activity. A colleague with whom I worked on a co-operative housing project years ago was surprised that I was opposed to abortion. He said to me: "I thought you were in favour of liberal causes." His remark shows the false paths we can take if we don't understand justice as informed by charity.

When we think of "charity" as the *virtue* of charity, which is at the heart of the Christian life, we can see why we have to be committed *both* to social action (the works of justice) and to social service (the works of charity). Unless we are ready to engage in social service, and prepared to give financial and personal assistance to those who are here and now suffering from hunger, or to visit the sick, welcome refugees, and so on, then we are not the sort of people who should think of undertaking social action, or the works of justice.

8. Charity or justice: social service or social action?

If we turn our attention now to justice, in the sense of the virtue of justice, a virtue that is motivated by Christian charity, we find that in Catholic social teaching it is often referred to as *social* justice, or in the case of Pope John XXIII, as "justice and equity." This meaning of justice is closely connected to the growing awareness, throughout the 19th and early 20th centuries, first, that much of the personal suffering experienced by people is caused by social and political *structures,* that is, laws, social arrangements, social practices, and second, that most of these can be changed.

The history of the Christian social movements in the 19th century is very revealing. Catholic organizations in France and Germany that were originally established simply to carry out the works of mercy began to see that they had to address the root causes of the misery they were trying to alleviate. The Protestant Social Gospel Movement in the United States spoke of the need for a Christian sociology, an expression that reflected its awareness that Christians need to understand, and sometimes work to change, the *social conditions* that lead to human suffering. This realization of the need for social justice reaches its most articulate expression in Catholic social teaching in the 1971 Synod document, *Justice in the World*, which makes the statement: "Action for the sake of justice and participation in the transformation of the world fully appear to us to be a constitutive element of the preaching of the gospel, that is, of the mission of the Church for the redemption of the human race and its liberation from every state of oppression."

What we call Catholic social teaching is that body of principles, that part of moral theology, that concerns working for social justice, or undertaking what is usually called social action. It is therefore distinct from the "works of charity" or social service. Sometimes, however, the works of justice and the works of charity, are *not* clearly distinguished. Why does this matter? There are several important reasons.

First, social service can obscure the need for social action because it can *absorb our energy*, and thus stand in the way of our seeing the underlying issues that need to be addressed. A practical example of this is the community's support of food banks. While food banks have been a much-needed source of assistance for many people, we have become used to them and rarely reflect on what a scandal it is that we need hundreds of food banks in a rich country like this. In 1970, there were no food banks in Canada. Our dependence on food banks today is a sign of some basic injustices in our society, like inadequate social assistance rates and a lack of affordable housing, and we need to address those issues.

Second, social service tends toward *paternalism*. While it may be necessary to lend people a helping hand, and to provide financial and material support, the danger is that we increase their dependence on us. Those who are involved in sponsoring refugee families have probably seen the effects of our over-eagerness to do practically everything for them.

Third, social service can play into the hands of *neo-conservative governments*. They can claim that caring for the needy and the poor is properly the work of volunteer groups, church organizations, charitable associations, and they can use this claim in order to ignore their responsibility for instituting the social programs required by social justice. Exactly this approach has been taken by some governments in Canada and the United States in the past twenty years. They have insisted that aiding the poor was the task of charitable and church groups, and they used this as a justification for cutting taxes, a step that, as we know, benefits the well-off much more than it does the poor. Moreover, they ignored the fact that the sheer dollar amount of what was needed to assist people struggling to live on reduced social assistance payments far outstripped the resources of churches and charities.

Fourth, exclusive involvement in social service can adversely affect our sense of the common good and result in our failing to take the *critical stance* we should toward certain government policies. Good works, in other words, can mute our voices, especially if governments make it easier in some way for us to do our good works, and if they publicly praise those good works. Recall the words of Dom Helder Camara, the late Archbishop of Olinda and Recife:

8. Charity or justice: social service or social action?

"When I give food to the poor, they call me a saint. When I ask why the poor have no food, they call me a communist."

Fifth, when Christians devote their efforts simply to social service and ignore social action, the *real movements* for social change that arise in a society tend to become *anti-religious* in character. They come to see Christian social service as undermining their efforts to bring about real social change. This has happened many times in the past 150 years. This also helps to explain the suspicion that some labour unions have toward churches.

Finally, perhaps most important, concentration simply on social service can, in the long run, *fail to serve the human person*. The ultimate aim of our efforts for others must be to enable them to develop as persons. Real development is always the development of persons. It is not just putting in water wells or building houses for people. It is enabling people to take control of their own lives.

What, finally, is the *ultimate* difference between charity and justice, between social service and social action? One answer is that social service is about helping *individuals,* while social action is about changing *society*. While this answer is correct, the difference goes much deeper.

Both social service and social action are about *evangelization*, or preaching the gospel. Social service preaches the gospel by serving as a *model* of how humans should act in the light of Christian revelation. Thus, Mother Teresa's homes for the dying or our own St. Vincent de Paul Societies announce the gospel simply by being there. They are living pictures of the gospel.

Social action however preaches the gospel by actively seeking to change culture so that it is more in accord with the gospel. Pope John Paul II wrote, "To teach and to spread her social doctrine pertains to the Church's evangelizing mission and is an essential part of the Christian message, since this doctrine points out the direct consequences of that message in the life of society ..." (*Centesimus Annus,* no. 5). This notion has gradually become more and more explicit in Catholic social statements over the past 50 years.

The documents of the Second Vatican Council, for example, picture the social order as an extension of the human person and so as something that has to be transformed by the gospel. Pope Paul VI and Pope John Paul II speak of the ways in which social structures and practices can solicit us into sinful ways of action and can also prevent us from doing the deeds of justice and charity. Indeed, they speak of the ways in which certain laws, social customs, and trade relations do our sinning for us. Pope Paul VI wrote, "For the Church is it a question not only of preaching the gospel in ever wider geographic areas or to ever-greater numbers of people, but also of affecting and as it were upsetting, through the power of the gospel, mankind's criteria of judgment, determining values, points of interest, lines of thought, sources of inspiration and models of life, which are in contrast with the word of God and the plan of salvation" (*Evangelii Nuntiandi*: no. 19).

The Second Vatican Council clearly related Christian social action to the mission of the Church: "Christ's work of redemption, which deals essentially with the salvation of people, embraces also the renewal of the entire temporal order." It goes on to say that the mission of the Church is "not only to bring Christ's message and his grace to people, but also to penetrate and perfect the temporal order with the gospel spirit" (*Decree on the Apostolate of the Laity,* no. 5). A respected commentator says that the second of these two tasks involves both the healing of those wounds in the temporal order that come from sin, and positive steps to help open this order to Christian values.

As one writer points out, the pastoral consequences of this view of social action are far-reaching. They mean we must balance our efforts to lead individuals to conversion with efforts to change social institutions. We must see our role as not only reconciling people in situations of conflict but also of sometimes making the painful decision to take sides in struggles for justice. We must bear witness in our lives to the reality of the spiritual world and the kingdom of God and yet also work for the transformation of this world.

8. Charity or justice: social service or social action?

Resources for Discussion:

Scripture: *Matthew* 22: 34-40

Social Documents: *Sollicitudo Rei Socialis*, no. 41

Questions for Discussion:

- Foodbanks are supported by many parishes today. Should we take a second look at that support and perhaps direct our energies more into changing the situations that make foodbanks necessary?

- Many works of charity derive financial support from charity bingos and other forms of gambling. Since addiction to gambling is a serious social problem, should we, as a matter of justice, get away from using funds raised in this way to support our charitable works?

- Can we think of instances in which we support and encourage some work of charity because in reality we lack the courage to tackle the deeper issues of justice that the situation involves?

- Do our works of charity sometimes accept funds from companies or groups which we ought to be challenging for their failures of justice?

9. "It's mine; I worked for it; I can do what I like with it!"

One of the first things we learn to say as children is, "It's mine!" As we get older we find ourselves speaking of "*my* hard-earned money". Money is simply a means of exchange, and so the real issue here is what we mean by referring to anything as *mine*. What do we mean by ownership and property? The word "property" comes from a Latin word, *proprius*, which means "one's own." Property is something external to me that I can say I "own."

In what sense is anything truly "mine?" Clearly, there is nothing in the natural world that had my name on it before I came on the scene. Nothing in the physical world belongs of its very nature to any one person. If we are going to speak of "natural ownership" of the physical world, then we must say that the only owner is God, for God created and sustains it.

The human relation to earthly goods is most properly called *stewardship*. The creation story represents God as saying: "Let us make humankind in our image, according to our likeness" *(Genesis* 1:26). We are *like God* in the sense that we are *self-directed*. We can manage our own lives and we can manage other things. We are *responsible* (that is, "answerable") for ourselves and other things. This is not true of any other creature on earth. That is why it is proper to see humans as the natural managers *or stewards* of the earth. All humans have a natural right to carry out that role of managing earthly goods.

Managing earthly goods involves caring for them and changing them so that they are ready for human use. Experience has shown that, in view of our common human weakness, the best way of doing this is by establishing a system of *private ownership*. This is the argument put forth by Aristotle and St. Thomas Aquinas. Taking people as they are, we find that under a system of private ownership the managing of earthly goods is more careful, more orderly, and more peaceful. Private ownership is what works, given the reality of human sinfulness. However such ownership is still a form of *stewardship*. Moreover, any given system of private ownership must be organized in such a way as to ensure that all people are able to exercise their natural right to manage earthly goods. This means that some particular systems of private property-holding are immoral because in practice they exclude large numbers of people from carrying out their natural role of being stewards of God's world.

In the 17th century, a new meaning of ownership began to appear. Some people began to speak of human work as the source of ownership. Property is seen as something produced by *my labour*. The argument goes that I own myself and my bodily powers, and so I own what is produced by those powers. Hence the view "It's mine; I worked for it; I can do what I like with it." Property becomes an extension of the human person, something to which I have an absolute right.

This line of thinking is wrong for several reasons. For one thing, it does not make sense to speak of "me" owning "myself" or "my bodily powers". The human person can be a *subject* of ownership, in the sense described above, but not an *object* of ownership. Moreover, my human labour would not be able to produce anything unless it made use of the goods of the earth (which are "owned" by God) and unless it was made possible by the presence of an organized society (which therefore has claims against what I have produced). Hence, Pope John Paul II wrote, "There is aways a social mortgage on all private property."

Two other observations should be made about human ownership.

First, the word "ownership" is *analogical*. In other words, it does not mean the same thing in every situation. I own my clothes in a more complete sense than I own a piece of real estate. The clothes are more closely associated with my person and have less impact on others than is the case with the real estate. Again, I own my house in a fuller sense than I own shares in a company. The social impact of my shares is greater than that of my house. The more anything I own touches on the lives of other people, the more society has the right to put limitations on my ownership.

Second, ownership is a *means to an end.* It is meant to protect and enhance human dignity. It is not an end in itself. In spite of the claims sometimes put forward in modern advertising, our human fulfillment does not come from ownership. It comes from carrying out our role as God's stewards or managers. In other words it comes from carrying out our particular "vocation" or "calling" in life.

There is another meaning of the word "property" that is not directly concerned with ownership. The term sometimes indicates a *place* of one's own. Our own place in the world does tend to have a personal, and sometimes even a sacred character to it. In the words of a contemporary philosopher, we "reverberate" with our own place in the world. The more property is looked upon in this way, the less it is regarded as an object of "ownership" that could be put up for sale. See the response of Naboth to the offer of Ahab who wanted to buy his family vineyard: "The Lord forbid that I should give you my ancestral inheritance" (*1 Kings,* 21:1-16).

9. "It's mine; I worked for it; I can do what I like with it!"

Resources for Discussion:

Scripture: *Genesis*: 1: 26-31

Social Documents: *Constitution on the Church in the Modern World*, no. 71

Questions for Discussion:

- Can you think of some particular systems of private property in some countries that should be judged immoral? Why are they immoral?

- What are some of the claims that organized society has on what I earn? How are these claims met?

- In what sense is it true to say that "my home is my castle"?

Suggested video to end the meeting:

Romero (Paulist Productions)

10. Making and spending money

Few things are as disconcerting as to hear grade school children say that what they want to do when they grow up is make a lot of money. Clearly, the society in which they live is forming them much more than is the gospel. What is the proper Christian attitude to money? We can speak of four principles.

First, it is proper, and often even required of us, to acquire whatever we need in order to carry out our particular role in God's world. This is the principle of *involvement*. Vatican II's *Constitution on the Church in the Modern World* sees most people called upon to be involved. The amount of money we try to have will vary according to our role. For example, people raising a family obviously need more money.

Second, we must see ourselves as *stewards* of what we possess rather than as absolute owners. We are *accountable* to God and to others for how we use our money and possessions. It is morally wrong to separate ownership from responsibility.

Third, we need to cultivate a spirit of *detachment*. Money is seductive. It easily steals our heart. One of the best remedies against this is to practise generosity, or what the great Christian thinkers call "liberality" (from the Latin, *liber*, meaning "free", because it helps us to maintain a spirit of freedom with respect to our money and possessions).

Fourth, we need to remember that, as followers of Jesus, we are called to be *witnesses*. Our use of money and goods should witness to gospel values, and should reflect, for example, our belief in eternal life, as well as our awareness that the poor of this world are our brothers and sisters.

A basic lesson of economics is that the items we purchase, and the businesses we patronize, represent choices we make from among different items we could have bought, and various businesses we could have dealt with. So, when we make our purchases, we cast a *money vote*, for certain products, for certain retailers, for certain manufacturers, and for certain values. Since that is the case, we need to take a careful look at who is profiting from our vote. Is it a business or a company whose activity respects human rights, for example? In short, what are the social consequences of the way we spend our money?

Before we make a purchase we should ask ourselves, "What were the circumstances under which this article was produced?" To take a practical example, let us say that the article was manufactured in China. There is a website entitled "Human Rights for Workers", maintained by a well-known American social activist, Robert Senser. On April 3, 2002, he sent the following letter to Sears, Roebuck and Co.:

"Imagine – my new Microwave Hood Combination made in the People's Republic of China! I discovered that disturbing fact when, a few days after this Kenmore product was installed, I peered at the label inside the door and discovered where it was manufactured. Actually, the label said it was 'made in PRC,' an abbreviation suggesting shyness about divulging the country of origin. One reason I avoid buying a product from China is I don't know whether it was made in one of China's many prison factories. I wonder whether you know. And further, I don't know whether the prisoners who made it were priests, nuns, or other political prisoners. I wonder whether you know. More generally, please tell me whether Sears, following the example of Reebok and some other multinationals, has a code of labor conduct covering your factories and suppliers in China. If so, please send me a copy. I wonder whether it forbids the use of priests, nuns, and other political prisoners in making your products, and whether you have a reliable system of monitoring compliance." To date, Mr. Senser has received no reply.

To be fair, a similar letter could have been written to Zellers, Canadian Tire, Wal-Mart, or many other retail giants.

The *New York Times Magazine* for March 3, 2002, carried a piece entitled "John Kamm's Third Way". This article refutes the argument that doing business with China is the best way to improve their human rights record. In fact, "far from raising standards in China, many companies with Chinese factories producing goods for American consumers are engaged in a race to the bottom. Investigators from Hong Kong and New York have found factories producing brand-name toys, clothing and shoes for the American market where the average wage was 14 to 19 cents an hour and where, during peak production seasons, workers had to be on the job for 15 hours a day, seven days a week" (p. 60).

Another question we should ask ourselves when we cast our *money vote* is, "What kind of employer is this company I am patronizing?" Katherine L. Hughes, a senior research associate for the Institute on Education and the Economy at Columbia University, wrote, in the March 3, 2002, issue of the *The New York Times*, a response to an earlier article about the giant merchandiser, Wal-Mart. The article, she pointed out, "did not mention a significant reason behind Wal-Mart's success: the company's overt anti-unionism and the low wages paid to its employees."

Consider too these comments that appeared in the September, 2001, issue of the *Globe and Mail Review of Business* Magazine, in regard to the fast food giant, McDonald's. The former labour relations chief of McDonald's Corp. is quoted as saying: "Unions are inimical to what we stand for and how we operate." The article goes on to show why. It is because the company has a "tradition of central control." (p. 40). That is why "Teenagers have been the perfect candidates for these jobs, not only because they are less expensive to hire than adults, but also because their youthful inexperience makes them easier to control." (p. 41)

Price and convenience should never be the over-riding consideration when we spend our money. We need to ask ourselves seriously, "What kind of a world am I voting for by the purchases I make?"

10. Making and spending money

Resources for Discussion:

Scripture: *Luke* 16: 1-15

Social Documents: *Justice in the World*, nos. 47-48

Questions for Discussion:

- Using the four gospel principles as guides, do you think there is a place in our society for rich people? For poor people?

- What can we do about products made in conditions that violate human rights?

- Do personal boycotts of businesses that treat employees unjustly do any good?

Suggested videos to end the meeting:

What's the Cost of Your Blouse? (Innerlight Productions, Oakland)

Tomorrow We Finish (Maryknoll)

11. Investing our money

The public scandals involving some major corporations, like Enron and Nortel, have made many people nervous about investing in the stock market. If the consequence of this is that people will now look more carefully at what they are doing when they invest their money, then that is a good outcome. Far too often, even conscientious Catholics have invested only with an eye to the expected rate of return.

A highly-respected Catholic economist, Charles Wilbur, reminds us, "The basic point made by Catholic social teaching is that investment should not be directed solely by private profit. Private investors need to balance individual profit with concern for the common good."

Catholic teaching on this topic rests on two principles.

The first is the principle of *stewardship*. Only God is an absolute owner. Human ownership is more properly referred to as *stewardship*. We have a right to make human use of the goods of this earth, but we are accountable to God and to others for *how* we use them. Ownership always involves responsibility. The two cannot, in good conscience, be separated.

The second is the principle of *investment*. People who invest their money in stocks become owners of the company in which they invest. Though they entrust the running of that company to others, they are still responsible for how their money is used. Because of the distance in a modern economy between investors and those entrusted with the investors' money, this is often a difficult principle to apply. It requires a diligent monitoring of the company's operation by the investor.

The U.S. Bishops put it clearly in their 1986 pastoral letter: "Individual Christians who are shareholders … must see to it that their invested funds are used responsibly…. As part-owners they must cooperate in shaping the policies of those companies through dialogue with management, through votes at corporate meetings, through the introduction of resolutions, and through participation in investment decisions" (*Economic Justice for All*, no. 354).

A British Catholic moralist, J. Mahoney, S.J., puts it this way: "Shareholders have moral responsibilities as the owners of a company." This raises the problem of "how to find ways of narrowing the gap between management and ownership and encourage a multitude of owners to recognise and exercise their moral responsibility for the behaviour of the company which they are financing and from which they profit."

This principle raises particular problems for those who choose to invest in mutual funds. It is difficult in such cases to know what companies one is involved with, since mutual fund managers regularly move investments around in their search for the best overall return. A few years ago, Canada's Foreign Affairs Minister admitted that "oil money from Calgary-based Talisman Energy's operations in Sudan is fueling a bloody civil war there." At the time, Talisman shares were widely-held by some of the largest mutual funds, in which many thousands of Canadians are investors. Talisman later sold its oil holdings in Sudan.

Some people try to carry out their responsibilities by seeking out so-called ethical funds, and entrusting them with their investments. But this solution is not as easy as it seems. For it depends on what criteria the fund managers are following in deciding what is ethical behaviour in a company. Some fund managers simply abstain from investing in companies that manufacture armaments or tobacco products, for example. Yet, what about the labour policies of a company, its attitude to unions, its record in dealing with women or minorities, its practice perhaps, of outsourcing to sweatshops in poor countries, etc.? There is not, at present, any truly satisfactory alternative to personal monitoring of one's stocks.

Suppose we lack the time and expertise to do such monitoring? One alternative is to invest in bonds. When we purchase a bond, the ownership of our money is transferred to the borrower. So we do not become a part-owner of the borrower's business. Our bond is a pledge on the part of the borrower to return the equivalent amount of money at some point, together with whatever we have lost by not having our money available to us in the meantime.

While we should exercise care in the purchase of bonds, and avoid lending money to businesses whose activity is reprehensible, we do not have to exercise the same same level of responsibility as in the case of stocks, since we are not owners of the business in which we hold bonds. In purchasing bonds, we may want to give special consideration to bonds that support public goods, like municipal and public utility bonds.

Another alternative is to invest in a democratic institution which provides us with the opportunity to make our voice heard. For example, if we invest in Canada Savings Bonds, we are actually investing in our country, and have the satisfaction of knowing that we can express our views on the governance of the country through the ballot box, or by contacting our M.P. or other elected representatives. We can also invest in a G.I.C. at a credit union. When we join a credit union, of course, we purchase shares and so become an owner. As such, we have the right to make our voice heard at the annual meeting, and to take our concerns to our branch council.

11. Investing our money

Resources for Discussion:

Scripture: *Matthew* 25: 14-30

Social Documents: *Quadragesimo Anno*, nos. 50-51; *Constitution on the Church in the Modern World*, no. 70

Questions for Discussion:

- Do most people invest money in some ways at some point in life? In what ways?

- Do you know about any "ethical funds"? Are you aware of what criteria they use in declaring particular investments "ethical"?

- How would you go about investigating the policies and behaviour of a company in which you were thinking of investing?

- Might we sometimes invest in a company, whose activity is unjust in some way, so we could then have the right as a shareholder to make our voice heard?

12. Tax cuts

In February, 1992, the federal government cancelled the Family Allowance Program, which had existed in Canada since 1945. This was a particularly significant event, because it marked the first time we actually abolished a universal social program in this country. It represented a radical change in our view of Canadian society. It also served as a signal that the *tax revolt* was succeeding in Canada.

The tax revolt movement opposes any new taxes, and seeks to reduce existing taxes substantially. It began in California in the 1970s.

One of the causes of the tax revolt was public cynicism about the effectiveness of government spending, a conviction that there was large-scale waste.

Another cause was a campaign waged by special-interest groups. Such groups are usually funded by big business and the better-off in our society. In Canada, those groups have been mainly the Vancouver-based Fraser Institute, the Ottawa-based Canadian Council of Chief Executives (formerly the Business Council on National Issues), and the Toronto-based National Citizens' Coalition.

Tax revolts usually have "populist" overtones, but they largely benefit the well-off, and do not bring much relief to people with modest incomes. They also reduce the tax base, and so limit a society's ability to provide public services and social programs to its citizens. The Fraser Institute's annual announcement of "tax freedom day," a date somewhere around mid-year when it says people have now finished working just to pay various taxes and will be "working for themselves" for the rest of the year, totally ignores the fact that our taxes pay for the public services all of us need and from which all of us benefit. As a result of various tax cuts, many services that were publicly-provided in the past now have to be paid for by private citizens. Education and health services, as well as recreational facilities, are obvious examples. This is not a big issue for the well-off, who generally prefer to buy their own services privately, but it is of immense importance to the rest of society.

Two facts should be kept in mind regarding the tax revolt. First, our present federal deficit in Canada is not primarily the result of government overspending. It was caused by the *undercollection* of taxes, especially in the 1970s when huge tax advantages were granted to large corporations and to the rich, things like the business entertainment tax deduction, and the family trusts deduction. It was also caused by the unprecedented interest rates of the early 1980s, when governments had to pay very high interest on such things as Canada Savings Bonds and Treasury Bills.

Second, Canada does not spend an exorbitant amount of its gross domestic product on social programs. In fact, we are below most other industrialized countries in this respect, and usually only the United States spends less on social programs than we do.

What does Catholic social teaching tell us about the tax revolt? First, it reminds us that we are not absolute owners of what we possess. Every owner is God's *tenant*: "The land shall not be sold in perpetuity, for the land is mine; with me you are but aliens and tenants" (*Leviticus* 25:23). Every owner, therefore, owes "taxes" to God's representatives, the poor: "Is not this the fast that I choose: … to share your bread with the hungry and bring the homeless poor into your house?"(*Isaiah* 58:6-7). So there are claims against whatever we possess, and those claims are mostly met through the payment of taxes. Second, we are not isolated individuals simply pursuing our private goals. We are part of a *social family*. We are tied to one another in dozens of ways, as fellow citizens of our province, our country and our world. So we have *responsibilities* to one another, and again these are met especially through our taxes. Third, it is necessary to maintain universal social programs, which provide services all of us can count on simply because we are part of the family. The alternatives to such programs are "targeted" programs, involving means testing, and two-tiered services, both of which discriminate against large numbers of family members and stigmatize particular groups of people.

What we need is not tax *revolt* but tax *reform*; not necessarily fewer taxes, but *fairer* taxes.

Resources for Discussion:

Scripture: *Matthew* 22: 15-22; *Romans* 13: 1-7

Social Documents: *Constitution on the Church in the Modern World*, no. 30

Questions for Discussion:

• Why was the cancellation of the Family Allowance Program a sign that the "tax revolt" was succeeding in Canada?

• What signs of the "tax revolt" do you see in our country today?

• In what ways do you think the present tax system in Canada is unfair?

13. Who are the poor?

The Bible has a lot to say about the poor. "Let there be no poor among you" (*Deut* 15:4). "There was not a needy person among them, for as many as owned lands or houses sold them and brought the proceeds of what was sold. They laid it at the apostles' feet and it was distributed to each as any had need" (*Acts* 4: 34-35).

The presence of poor people in our world is a scandal to the Christian conscience, and a situation that we must struggle to correct.

Yet, an important question is, Who are the poor? We recognize without much difficulty the extremely poor people in Third World countries. About 800 million people in those countries live in conditions of complete destitution, barely able to survive from one day to the next. But what about the poor in our own country? Who are *they*?

According to most measures of poverty in Canada, the poor are those who lack what they require for physical survival (*absolute* poverty) and for social survival (*relative* poverty). The Canadian Council on Social Development considers a family of three persons living on an income that is 50% or less of the average family income in Canada to be poor. Statistics Canada publishes Low Income Cut-Off lines that are somewhat less generous but follow the same general principle. Other poverty lines of the same nature are the Social Planning Council of Metropolitan Toronto Budget Guide and the Guidelines of the Social Planning and Research Council of B.C. The sole example of an organization in Canada offering poverty guidelines that reflect only *absolute poverty* is the Fraser Institute in British Columbia.

What does the public think? Well, each year the Gallup polling organization asks Canadians what they believe is the least amount of money a family of four needs each week to get along. Regularly the answer people give agrees with the amount arrived at by Statistics Canada's Low Income Cut-Off Lines. Clearly, most Canadians see poverty as involving both absolute and relative poverty. Using that definition, 22.4% of Canadian households lived in poverty in 1997. In 1998, 19% of Canadian children were poor, one of the worst rates among industrialized nations.

Consider what *relative poverty* means. It means lacking the education, training, and ready cash to take advantage of good shopping buys; lack of access to credit; sending children to schools that are attuned to the middle class (poor parents can't afford to put their children into organized sports, for example); less access to health and medical services, etc. Relative poverty means less involvement in community organizations and activities. It brings with it a sense of exclusion, alienation, and helplessness.

Another way to look at relative poverty is to see it as reflecting the serious inequality in the distribution of total national income. For the past 50 years the lowest one-fifth of the Canadian population has received approximately 4.5% of the national income, while the top one-fifth has received approximately 43% of this income. That sort of inequality (10-1) creates huge social distances in Canadian society, and translates into enormous differences in social, economic and political power within our country. In 2001, CEO's of major corporations in the U.S. made 411 times as much as the average factory worker. By contrast, within the Mondragon Co-operatives that involve about 50,000 people in Spain, the rule is that no person makes more than three times the wage or salary of any other person.

To put a financial face on relative poverty, consider these figures published by the Ontario Social Safety Network for the year 2001. The maximum monthly amount a single person received from welfare in Ontario for shelter was $325, but the average monthly cost of a bachelor apartment in Ontario was $561. The amount, once rent and food are paid, that a single parent on social assistance with one child had for all other expenses, per person, per day, was $2.24. It is no wonder that there are about 270 foodbanks in Ontario alone, and that their use is growing.

Our attitude toward the poor may be influenced by inaccurate information or stereotypes. Facts like the following should be publicized widely: (1) More than 30% of all poor families are in the workforce; they are not on welfare, but are working for inadequate wages. (2) The majority of unemployed people would prefer to work — every serious study has revealed this — but steady work is not available to them for one reason or another. (3) About two-thirds of the people on social assistance have no alternative; some physical or social disability, or the need to care for very young children, keeps them there. (4) Every serious study reveals that the percentage of cheaters in the welfare system is about 5% — much lower than the rate of cheating among the well-off in our society!

Resources for Discussion:

Scripture: *Amos* 8: 4-8; *James* 2: 1-7

Social Documents: *Mater et Magistra*, no. 150; *Octogesima Adveniens*, nos. 10-11

Questions for Discussion:

• What do you believe are the principal causes of poverty in our country? In our community?

• What proportion of a person's income should be devoted to shelter? What proportion of their income do most welfare recipients in our cities devote to shelter today?

14. Third world debt: a moral issue

In 1981 a family in P.E.I., who had been paying their mortgage for five years, still owed $20,966.20. That year, they had to refinance the mortgage. The bank would agree only to a one-year arrangement, at the prevailing rate of 21.5%. For a full year, they made monthly payments of $386.00. By year's end, they had paid the bank a total of $4,632.00, which covered $4,592.93 in interest and $39.07 on the principal. However the bank also charged a $50.00 fee for re-financing. So, after a year of paying all that money, the family was actually $10.93 worse off financially than it had been at the start of the year. This true example helps us to understand the situation in which most of the world's poor nations find themselves.

In 1995, Third World countries owed more than two trillion dollars (U.S.) to foreign creditors. About $325 billion of this amount was owed to multilateral institutions like the World Bank, the International Monetary Fund and Regional Development Banks. "From 1980 until 2003, the external debts of all developing countries have grown from US$554 billion to US$2.4 trillion. This fourfold increase occurred despite the fact these countries have made US$5.2 trillion in debt payments over the intervening 23 years" (Kairos, *Global Economic Justice Report*, Oct. 2004, p. 5).

How did things get so bad?

First, most experts agree that it began to get really bad in 1971 when the U.S. government unilaterally repudiated some of the features of the 1945 Bretton Woods Agreement, according to which all other countries' currencies were measured in terms of U.S. dollars, which in turn was tied to gold at $35.00 (U.S.) per ounce. The U.S. action caused a loss of value in many poor countries' currencies.

Second, in 1973, OPEC dramatically increased the price of oil. Most poor countries suffered from this. The countries that prospered from it deposited their new wealth in rich countries' banks.

Third, those banks embarked on aggressive lending policies encouraging poor countries to borrow money. The banks did not properly investigate to see how such borrowed money would be spent; money was loaned without qualms to dictators; much was spent for arms, or on ill-considered projects; much was simply wasted or found its way into dishonest pockets.

Fourth, in 1979, OPEC again raised the price of oil. Rich countries raised interest rates to protect their economies. This caused a drop in demand for exports from poor countries and a decline in their value, thus plunging those countries further into debt.

Fifth, in 1982, Mexico threatened to default on its massive debt. Rich countries, alarmed that this might start a world-wide default, poured money into multilateral institutions like the World Bank and the International Monetary Fund. These institutions then began making large loans to poor countries so they could continue paying the interest on their debt. As a condition of such loans, poor countries were required to accept Structural Adjustment Programs which obliged those countries to cut back severely on social programs, like health and education. The result for the daily life of ordinary people in those countries has been devastating.

In 2000, "severely indebted low-income countries paid out US$ 14.4 billion more in interest and principal ... than they received in new loans." (Kairos, *Global Economic Justice Report* (Vol. 2, No. 3, July 2003). So the present arrangement is literally draining the lifeblood of poor countries. The poor of our world are subsidizing the rich of our world with their lives and the lives of their children. Essentially the poor countries have gone bankrupt. Their debts are unpayable. Yet there is no legislation to protect them from their creditors.

The international *Jubilee Proposal* was for a one-time write-off of the debt of the 32 poorest countries in the world. This proposal was, and still is, strongly supported by many groups, including churches, and by the Canadian Conference of Catholic bishops. Canada has responded by writing off a considerable amount of money that was owed to our government and its various agencies. But we need to keep two things in mind. *First*, in recent years, Canada has cut back severely on the amount of aid that it provides for poor countries; at present we devote only about 0.25% of our GDP to this purpose, in spite of a pledge made thirty years ago to provide 0.70%. *Second,* what is most needed is a truly generous forgiveness plan by the multilateral institutions like the World Bank. Canada is a player in such institutions, and needs to be a courageous voice in their meetings.

"Do not exploit the poor because they are poor and do not crush the needy in court, for the Lord will take up their case and will plunder those who plunder them" (*Proverbs* 22:22-23). "They trample on the heads of the poor as upon the dust of the ground and they deny justice to the oppressed" (*Amos* 2:7). "Forgive us our debts, as we have also forgiven our debtors" (*Matthew* 6:12).

14. Third world debt: a moral issue

Resources for Discussion:

Scripture: *Luke* 16: 19-31

Social Documents: *Populorum Progressio*, nos. 47-48. *Sollicitudo Rei Socialis*, no. 32

Questions for Discussion:

- Some Catholic writers today take the position that much of the Third World debt is unjust and so should not be paid. Why would they say this? What do you think?

- Why do you think Canada's foreign aid budget continues to be so low?

- What are some things our country can do to improve the situation of poor countries?

Suggested videos to end the meeting:

Banking on Life and Debt (Maryknoll)

A Piece of the Pie (Twenty-Third Publications)

15. Co-operatives and credit unions

One of our Canadian Catholic folk heroes is Father Moses Coady, the priest who served as the guiding spirit of the co-operative movement at St. Francis Xavier University in Antigonish, N.S., during the '30s, '40s and '50s. He was the inspiration for the 1953 decision to establish a credit union in each parish of London Diocese. Today, it is often people trained at the Coady Institute in Antigonish who guide the micro-credit co-operatives that are such a godsend in poor countries. In India, hundreds of such micro-credit co-operatives have been established with the assistance of Save A Family Plan, which is based at St. Peter's Seminary in London.

Co-operatives and credit unions first arose in the 19th century in reaction to the dominant economic and social views of the day. In the economic literature of 19th century England, the person was pictured as a rugged individual, predominantly selfish by nature, who finds fulfillment in possessions. The economy was viewed primarily as a fierce competition among such individuals. In vivid contrast to these views, promoters of co-operatives and credit unions saw persons as naturally social beings, who find fulfillment in "being" rather than "having", and who are called to be masters of their destiny. The economy, they felt, should reflect the fact that it is more natural for human beings to co-operate than to compete, and should be characterized by democratic institutions through which people are able to participate actively in economic life.

Much of the inspiration for co-ops and credit unions came from the ideas of Robert Owen, born in Wales in 1771. Owen, a successful businessman and a member of parliament, promoted social legislation and trade unions, and started "model" factories and communes. Many of his social experiments failed, however, because Owen relied too exclusively on social structures and education to change people, and neglected the role of religious conviction and practice.

15. Co-operatives and credit unions

In 1843, one of the groups inspired by Owen began to meet in Rochdale, England, an area of severe economic distress. These "Rochdale Pioneers" led by Charles Howarth, began the co-operative and credit union movement. They formulated the *Rochdale Principles*, which today form the basis of all credit unions and co-operatives.

The most important of the Rochdale principles are: (1) A co-operative society is to be democratically-controlled, which means "one member, one vote," no matter how many shares a member may own. (2) Money invested in capital in a co-operative is to receive interest at no more than the prevailing rate. (3) The net profit is to be returned to the members of the co-operative or credit union. (4) There is to be open membership. (5) Political and religious freedom is to be observed for all members. (6) All business is to be done for cash, to encourage members to live within their income. (7) Funds are to be set aside regularly for the education of the members. (8) All employees are to be fairly treated. (9) Co-operatives are to co-operate with one another.

Co-operatives spread to Belgium in 1880, to France in 1885, to Germany in the 1890s, and then rapidly to other countries. In Canada, the Stellarton Co-operative Society was founded in Nova Scotia in 1861.

The credit union movement in North America was founded by Alphonse Desjardins, who established his first *caisse populaire* at Lévis, Quebec, in 1900. He drew on European ideas such as those of a Protestant social thinker named Friedrich Wilhelm Raiffeisen (1818-88). Desjardins was later honoured by Pope Pius X for his work.

Catholic social teaching has long supported and encouraged co-ops and credit unions. They are institutions that promote the principle of solidarity by providing a practical way to take action together for the good of the whole. They also reflect the principle of subsidiarity because they are instruments of self-help. Pope Leo XIII, in his 1891 encyclical *Rerum Novarum*, defended the right of association and promoted the principle of self-help. Pope John XXIII spoke warmly of credit unions in his 1961 letter, *Mater et Magistra*.

Pope Paul VI addressed the World Congress of Agricultural Co-operatives in 1972. The Bishops' Conferences of both Canada and the United States have several times expressed strong support for co-operatives and credit unions. In their 1950 pastoral letter, the Quebec Bishops saw co-operatives and credit unions as "instruments of education and means of amending our economic system." (*The Problem of the Worker in the light of the Social Doctrine of the Church,* no. 117).

These institutions deserve our support, because they foster a spirit of working together and helping one another, and they give people some genuine control over the financial institutions that so affect their lives, because the members of these institutions own them.

Resources for Discussion:

Scripture: *I Corinthians* 12: 12-31

Social Documents: *Mater et Magistra*, nos. 146-148

Questions for Discussion:

• Why should Catholics make a special effort to support co-operatives and credit unions?

• What is your assessment of the way in which Canada's major chartered banks have operated in recent decades?

• Some people have started such things as co-operative grocery stores. In what areas of the economy would you like to see more co-operatives?

Suggested video to end the meeting:

Moses Coady (National Film Board of Canada)

16. Subdue the earth or protect it?

Fifty years ago a large industrial plant, spewing black smoke into the sky, was a proud symbol of progress. Today that same plant is denounced as a merchant of death in our environment. The question raised by environmentalists today is: Why does Western culture act in such a manipulative way toward nature? Why does it take such an exploitative approach to the animal kingdom? Some people actually blame the Bible, and Christianity, for the harm that "progress" has done to our planet. They say it is because the Bible teaches humans to "subdue the earth" (*Genesis* 2:28). They say it is also because Christianity teaches the superiority of humans over other types of life. How should we answer the charges that Christianity is anti-environmental? There are three points.

First, the attitude which looks upon the world as more or less an object to be manipulated by us, and as a reality that is totally subject to our human will, is an attitude that dates from about the fourteenth century. Moreover, it springs from several causes, none of which is specifically Christian. It was late medieval writers who first pictured the world as an "object" to be "dominated" by human "subjects," and who spoke of humans as "wills" that stand over the world to make it answer "our" questions and serve "our" purposes. The philosopher, René Descartes (1596-1650) began his investigation of reality not with nature but with a subjective "I" that summons all of nature before it as its "object". The philosopher and scientist Francis Bacon (1561-1626) ushered in the modern scientific mentality when he declared that "knowledge is power."

Second, the Catholic Church has always taught that our attitude toward our world should be one of *stewardship* rather than *domination*. Moreover, for more than 30 years now, since environmental awareness has become more widespread, Vatican documents have been among the first to speak of the misuse of the environment as a moral issue. Pope Paul VI warned against "an ill-considered exploitation of nature", and spoke of it as "a wide-ranging social problem which concerns the entire human family" (*Octogesima Adveniens*, no. 21).

In that same year, the Catholic Bishops gathered in Rome for their Synod gave strong support to the Stockholm Conference on the Environment. On January 1, 1990, Pope John Paul offered a profound Christian reflection on the environmental crisis in his Message for the World Day of Peace.

Third, Pope John Paul II reminded us of what the *Book of Genesis* means when it calls on humans to "subdue the earth", to "dominate" it, to "exercise dominion" over it. *Genesis* pictures the human person as the one who can stand before God and speak with God. On our earth, only humans can do this; only humans can come to *understand* nature to some degree, and can come to recognize the God from whom it all came. Only humans, then, can use nature to honour God. Humans, possessed of intelligence and the power of self-direction, are in fact the "image" of God. That is the reason why God, in *Genesis*, can call on humans to share in God's providential care of the world. Human work, then, is intended by God to be a *sharing in God's activity* and dominion over the world. (Because the Latin word for Lord is *Dominus*, this human sharing in God's activity is called *dominion*.) So humans are called to "subdue the earth" in such a way that it will serve God's purposes. Precisely because human work is a sharing in the Lord's management, it must seek out and support God's intentions in nature. There could be no greater call to environmental concern than this. Hence the Pope says, "When it comes to the natural world, we are subject not only to biological laws but also to moral ones" (*The Social Concern of the Church,* no.34).

16. Subdue the earth or protect it?

Resources for Discussion:

Scripture: *Psalms 19, 65, 104.*

Social Documents: *Sollicitudo Rei Socialis*, no. 34

Questions for Discussion:

- Some environmentalists speak as if the world would be better off without humans. What is your reaction to that view?

- The 1987 U.N. Bruntland Report spoke of the earth as filled with environmental time bombs. What are some of those "bombs"? Do you think most of us are aware of them?

- What are some of the ways in which each of us can be more environmentally conscious?

17. Immigrants: a threat or a blessing?

An anti-immigrant mentality prevails in much of Western Europe today, and lately there are signs of a similar attitude gaining ground in Canada. For example, the "Safe Third Country Agreement" signed by the United States and Canada in the closing days of 2002, is widely viewed by human rights groups as creating serious obstacles for refugees seeking to enter Canada. Moreover, a senior federal government official recently repeated the statement "Immigration to Canada is a privilege and not a right." I say "repeated", because this was the position put forward by Prime Minister Mackenzie King in a famous speech in 1947, and quoted approvingly by a Minister of Immigration in the 1960s.

Yet the statement is clearly false! Article 13 of the United Nations *Declaration of Human Rights* recognizes the *natural right* of all people to freedom of movement within their own country and between countries. Pope John XXIII clearly enunciated this right also: "Again every human being has the right to freedom of movement and of residence within the confines of his own state. When there are just reasons in favour of it, he must be permitted to emigrate to other countries and take up residence there. The fact that he is a citizen of a particular state does not deprive him of membership in the human family, nor of citizenship in that universal society, the common, world-wide fellowship of men" (*Pacem in Terris* no. 25*).

Like most other rights, especially those involving the use of finite earthly resources, the right to migrate is subject to the requirements of the common good. Yet, as Pope Pius XII insisted in 1952, the grave need of so many people to migrate should not be obstructed by an overly-restrictive interpretation of this limitation. In fact, in view of the reluctance of richer nations like our own to promote the development of poorer countries through adequate trade and aid policies, we should recognize that we have no moral alternative but to admit more people from countries mired in poverty. Moreover, countries like our own, that boast of their respect for human rights, cannot ignore the millions of refugees in our world who seek only the opportunity to live a decent life. As Pope John Paul II pointed out, most people would prefer to remain in their own country. Yet if the international community cannot succeed in creating a political and economic climate in which all countries can prosper, then that community must be open to larger migration movements (*On Human Work* (no. 23).

Christians should be, and often are, a major voice in favour of immigrants and refugees. After all, the notions of "deliverance" and "liberation" are integral to our faith. Moroever the call to identify with the poor and homeless is forcefully put in St. Matthew's picture of the last judgment (Chapter 25). The Book of Revelation also pictures the "New Jerusalem", that rich symbol of our eternal home, as a city open on every side, welcoming people from every nation, an image that surely rules out an overly-protective "stockade" mentality on our part. In his message for the 2003 World Day of Migrants and Refugees, Pope John Paul II said that a mix of ethnic backgrounds, languages and customs is "a mark of the Church, expressing her essential openness to all that is the work of the Spirit in every people."

Several objections to a generous immigration and refugee policy tend to be repeated from time to time, even though they have been shown, again and again, to lack foundation. One objection is that immigration is likely to lead to overcrowding. The obvious response to this is that Canada's very low birth-rate and aging population has created a situation in which we are in serious need of more immigrants than we are presently receiving. (We must also keep in mind that, every year, about 55,000 people leave Canada for another country).

It is also claimed that more immigration will exacerbate our unemployment rate. In fact, though several serious studies have been done on this topic, no major relationship between the rates of immigration and of unemployment has ever been established. Immigrants often take jobs that no one else wants. Many of them bring with them skills that our economy needs. Most of all, immigrants require goods and services, and so they cause a rise in demand in our economy. That, in turn, creates jobs.

Finally, "national security" fears are sometimes at the root of anti-immigration attitudes. During the "cold war" this was reflected in the greater ease with which people fleeing communist regimes were admitted to Canada, while those suffering oppression from right wing governments had a much harder time getting in. At the present time there are certainly valid grounds for our fear of admitting terrorists. We need good intelligence and screening networks. Yet in the long run it will be by protecting human rights, including the right of freedom of movement for all people, that we will help to create a more humane world, one in which there will be less excuse for terrorism to exist.

17. Immigrants: a threat or a blessing?

Resources for Discussion:

Scripture: *Matthew* 25: 31-46

Social Documents: *Laborem Exercens*, no. 23

Questions for Discussion:

- People in many countries worry that increased immigration is going to change the character of their society — for example, societies that have traditionally seen themselves as "Christian" or "Judaeo-Christian". Is this a legitimate concern?

- Some farming areas of our country bring in migrant labourers for the growing or harvesting season, but such workers are then required to return home at the end of the season. What is your reaction to this practice?

- Do you think Catholics in our part of the world are sufficiently open to sponsoring refugees?

Suggested videos to end the meeting:

Who Gets In? (National Film Board of Canada)

Starting Over: Refugee Voices (Citizenship and Immigration Canada)

18. Crime and punishment

On July 9, 2000, Pope John Paul II paid a visit to a large prison in Rome, where he spoke to the prisoners and staff. It was part of his observance of the Jubilee Year, and so he used the occasion to make some fundamental statements about the Christian approach to crime and punishment. In particular he made three points.

First, every prisoner, no matter who he or she may be, or what the circumstances are, is still a person created in the image and likeness of God. Each prisoner is someone whom Christ the Good Shepherd searches out, and someone whom he accompanies on his or her journey. So the dignity and human rights of every prisoner must be respected. It is never permissible to subject prisoners to inhuman conditions, or to discrimination and violence.

Second, time in prison should be, above all, a time of restoration. Jailers are not the masters of a prisoner's time; God is. So the prisoner should see this as a time to rebuild relations with God and others. There should be contact with family, and a readiness to engage in works of solidarity with others. The jailer should see it as a time for the training and treatment that will make possible a prisoner's successful re-entry into society.

Third, authorities should continue to look for other forms of punishment that can serve as alternatives to imprisonment.

The pope's message reflects classic Catholic teaching on crime and punishment. St. Thomas Aquinas distinguishes *two* kinds of punishment: retrospective and prospective (*Summa Theol.* II-II, 108, 1).

Restrospective punishment is a form of revenge. Such punishment is not permitted to humans. "Vengeance is mine, says the Lord" (*Deut.* 32:35), and it is always forbidden to us. Moreover, a spirit of revenge always does great harm to us as persons. "Do not be overcome by evil, but overcome evil with good" (*Romans* 12:21).

18. Crime and punishment

Prospective punishment is pragmatic; it looks to the good that can be accomplished. Such good might be medicinal (the conversion or rehabilitation of the criminal), surgical (the removal of a very dangerous person from society), or deterrent (the sending of a message to others who might be thinking of committing crime). Only prospective punishment is legitimate for human beings to carry out.

In the light of this classic Catholic teaching, we can understand better the Church's stand on capital punishment. That stand is expressed in Pope John Paul II's 1995 encyclical letter:

"It is clear that, for these purposes to be achieved, the nature and extent of the punishment must be carefully evaluated and decided upon, and ought not go to the extreme of executing the offender except in cases of absolute necessity: in other words, when it would not be possible otherwise to defend society. Today however, as a result of steady improvements in the organization of the penal system, such cases are very rare, if not practically non-existent" (*The Gospel of Life*, no. 56).

When the debate on capital punishment took place in Canada, in the early 1970s, the Churches pointed out that our public policy as a society should always send the message that we value life. Moreover, we should never put an end to the possibility of conversion in the offender. We need also to be aware of the ever-present possibility of executing an innocent person. In Canada the cases of Donald Marshall (wrongly imprisoned for eleven years) and David Milgaard (wrongly jailed for 23 years) are frightening reminders of such a possibility. Other people also pointed to careful studies showing that capital punishment is not a stronger deterrent to crime than a long prison sentence. In fact, since capital punishment was abolished in Canada in 1976, our national homicide rate has actually declined.

A United Church of Canada Task Force on Penal Reform in 1977 pointed out that "in an individualistic society, we often fail to acknowledge our common life with one another … The accused person is processed through the system as an isolated wrongdoer … The result is that we fail to see ourselves in community solidarity with that person; and we fail to recognize our collective part in the social breakdown resulting in his/her behaviour."

Resources for Discussion:

Scripture: *Matthew* 5: 38-42; *Acts* 16: 23-34

Social Documents: *Pacem in Terris*, nos. 146-147

Questions for Discussion:

- What are we to think of the "Get tough on crime" mentality?
- What are some of the alternatives to prison that might have a place in our justice system?
- What attitude should we take to mega-prisons and to privately-operated prisons?

Suggested video to end the meeting:

Murder Remembered (National Film Board of Canada)

19. Work: just a job or something more?

During one of my summers as a university student I worked on the railroad. The foreman on one of my shifts was a foul-mouthed, inconsiderate man, whom it was difficult to respect. One day, when I was on a different shift, I was asked to deliver some documents to his home. When I met him in his home environment I could hardly believe it was the same man. He had a wife and family. He was polite and considerate. He received me with courtesy. It is experiences like this, I suspect, that lead us at times to regard the world of work as just a necessary evil, something we have to endure in order to make the money that will allow us to have a real life when we go home. What is the correct attitude to work then? Is work simply a necessary condition of that real life after work, or is it an essential ingredient of what should be considered a real life?

For Karl Marx, the answer was clear. For him, work was essential to what it means to be a human being. He defined humans as "animals that work," for only humans form a plan in their head, and use that plan to change nature; they can even change that plan, and so are capable of progress. Thus, Marx saw in work the means by which human beings can achieve freedom and fulfillment.

Pope John Paul II is in surprising agreement with Marx. "Only humans work," he points out. He goes on to state that "work is a good thing for persons – a good thing for their humanity – because through work, persons not only transform nature, adapting it to their own needs, but they also achieve fulfillment as human beings" (*On Human Work*, no. 9).

There is, however, an important difference between the pope and Marx. The pope insists that the human person is by nature a worker because the human person is the image of God. As God exercises a universal providence over all things, so God has made human beings in God's image so that they, in God's name, can exercise a sort of providential care over God's world.

They are to do this especially through work. To appreciate the pope's point better, it helps to consider three different pictures of work that were outlined by Robert Bellah, a prominent religious sociologist. Bellah says we may look upon what we do as a job, as a career, or as a calling.

First, it is possible to regard work simply as *a job.* Many employers and employees regard work in this way. This reduces work to a means for getting things done, or for making money. Even worse, it reduces work to the level of a *commodity*, that is, to something that is *sold* to the highest bidder in the marketplace, much as raw materials are treated. This vision of work has always been rejected by Catholic social teaching as unworthy of a human society.

Second, it is also possible to look upon work as *a career.* This view has much to be said for it, since it looks to the good of the worker, and to his or her fulfillment. It also usually involves a pursuit of excellence in what one does. But this view carries with it some dangers. For one thing, it can promote a self-centered mentality, a concentration on *my* private good, *my* career, *my* personal satisfaction. For another, it can lead to a compulsive approach to work, to work as something all-encompassing, so that one's life practically becomes one's work.

Third, it is possible to look upon work as *a vocation* or *calling.* This is the vision promoted by Catholic social teaching. Our work is our way of carrying out our role as the image of God; it is our way of caring for God's world, as God's manager. It is in this sense that the pope says there is a universal call to work. God calls all of us to some form of work (taking the word "work" in a fairly wide sense) in the sense that God calls all of us to the dignity of caring for God's world, as God's representatives.

When we look upon work as our calling, two important consequences become clear. First, we now see that "the basis for determining the value of human work is not primarily the kind of work being done but the fact that the one doing it is a person" (*On Human Work, no. 6*). Moreover, we also see that persons have a right to gainful work. An economy that does not make it possible for all who want gainful work to have it, is to that extent an unjust economy.

To see work as our calling is to open up a whole new vision of the greatness of work. For good work can build up our world, and in fact turn it into a home. It can also build up society, enabling human minds and hearts to flourish. It also has the potential to build up the individual worker, as it takes us out of ourselves and allows our human powers to mature. Good work can also help to redeem our world, as we bring the light of the gospel to the workplace, raising questions, transforming relationships, and giving new meaning even to the suffering and pain of work.

All of this has been a description of how we should *picture* work. Unfortunately, when we look at the real world of work around us, we are dismayed at a globalization process that gives a whole new meaning to "reducing work to a commodity," as huge companies contract out work to poor countries where people labour long hours, in inhuman conditions for meager wages. In our own country many people find employment opportunities scarce. Much of the work that is available is of the part-time and low-wage variety. It is clear that we not only have to revise the way we *picture* work, but also have to join the struggle to change the world of work.

Resources for Discussion:

Scripture: *Mark* 6: 1-3; *Colossians* 3: 23-24

Social Documents: *Laborem Exercens*, no. 6; *Constitution on the Church in the Modern World*, no. 35

Questions for Discussion:

- Humans are "animals that work". Yet don't horses work? Don't bees and ants work? (We speak of "workhorses" and "worker bees")

- Work is, or should be, the means to human freedom and fulfillment? Do you see work this way?

- We believe that work is a universal calling. What about those who cannot work, such as disabled people? What about students in school? What is the impact on unemployed people?

- "The basis for determining the value of human work is not primarily the kind of work being done, but the fact that the one doing it is a human person." What consequences do you see arising from this statement?

20. Work can be hazardous to your health

On a regular basis we see news items about workers killed or seriously injured in industrial accidents. It may be a mine disaster, or an equipment failure on a construction site, or the accidental release of toxic fumes. For many people, the only hint of any sort of danger in the workplace comes from such highly visible tragedies. Most of us do not realize how widespread is the danger to health and life in the workplace *every day*. In any given year in Canada, nearly twice as many hours of work are lost because of job-related injuries than result from all the strikes in the country put together. In Ontario alone, the number of workers injured on the job each year is measured in the hundreds of thousands, and the number killed is measured in the hundreds.

There are also the *hidden* hazards of the workplace, whose effects do not show up until many years have passed: cancer-causing substances, dangerous chemicals, harmful agents like mercury, lead, arsenic. One of the reasons why the United Farm Workers called for a boycott of California grapes for a number of years was to protest against the use of cancer-causing pesticides which endangered the lives of those working in the fields. Some people too are exposed to unusual stress that may ultimately take a terrible toll.

Danger in the workplace has long been a concern of Catholic social teaching. Pope Pius XI, in 1931, used graphic imagery to make the point, when he said that far too often "from the factory dead matter goes out improved, whereas men are there corrupted and degraded." The Second Vatican Council declared that "any way of organizing and directing" economic activity, "which might be detrimental to any workingmen and women would be wrong and inhuman." Pope John Paul said, in his letter on human work, that among the rights of working people "there should never be overlooked the right to a working environment and to manufacturing processes which are not harmful to the workers' physical health or to their moral integrity." (no. 19). More than once, the Canadian Catholic Bishops have insisted that it is a terrible perversion when the rights of labour are ignored or violated in the name of profit. In today's highly competitive global economy, where companies, for the sake of increasing their profit margin, outsource many tasks to non-union operations, the workplace often becomes a more dangerous place than ever. This is because, without the vigilance of a union, a company can more easily sacrifice safety to profit, especially if that company is located in a third world country.

Most jurisdictions in Canada now have legislation on health and safety that incorporates three rights of workers: the right to refuse hazardous work; the right to be informed about workplace hazards; and the right to be represented by a joint labour-management committee in decisions regarding the workplace environment. It is one thing, however, to have legislation on the books; it is quite another thing to have it enforced. There is inadequate monitoring of the workplace by government inspectors, while corners are being cut for the sake of financial gain. Even when improper conditions have been identified, foot-dragging can go on for months. In practice, workers are often forced to work in situations that are dangerous and life-threatening, daily afraid of being injured, and yet equally afraid of being fired if they speak out against a health hazard.

Workers need support in dealing with the hazards of the workplace. Thankfully, we now have The Canadian Centre for Occupational Health and Safety, located in Hamilton, Ont. This is a wonderful resource, jointly operated by business and labour. It maintains a very helpful website at www. ccohs.ca. In addition there are Occupational Health and Safety Organizations in a number of Canadian cities. It is an important act of respect for human dignity to support the work of such organizations.

Working people are not expendable. As Pope John Paul II says: "In the final analysis it is always the person who is the purpose of the work, whatever work it is that is being done." (*On Human Work, no. 6).*

Resources for Discussion:

Scripture: *Matthew* 7:12

Social Documents: *Constitution on the Church in the Modern World*, no. 67; *Laborem Exercens*, no. 19.

Questions for Discussion:

- Why do workplace injuries and deaths receive less publicity than strikes?
- Do you think workers' rights in regard to health and safety are being properly enforced in the workplaces you know about?

Suggested video to end the meeting:

Westray (National Film Board of Canada)

21. Labour unions

According to a report in the *New York Times*, union membership in the United States in the year 2000 stood at only 13.5% of the workforce, down from a peak of 35% in 1955. In Canada, the Canadian Labour Congress website states that union membership in Canada is presently 30% of the workforce; this is down from a high of 39% in 1980. Some people might welcome this downward trend in union membership. But no one who cares about human dignity, and certainly no committed Christian, should see these figures as anything but bad news.

In 1986, the Canadian Conference of Catholic Bishops published a statement entitled *Supporting Labour Unions—a Christian Responsibility*. This document, which faithfully reflects the official position of Catholic social teaching for more than 100 years, calls on us not only to tolerate unions, but also to support and encourage them. In fact, even Canadian civil law, prior to restrictive measures introduced recently by some provincial legislatures, reflected the conviction that union organizing represented a social good, and so should be facilitated by legislation. Why should unions be regarded as a social good? There are several reasons.

First, because unions give people a voice. In Catholic social thought, a healthy society is one in which the various groups of people are able to participate and to have input into social decisions and policy. The image most often used is that of the human body, in which the different organs have their own unique function, such as feet for walking, eyes for seeing, etc. Unions enable workers to have a collective voice in society, and to have input into the shape our society takes, just as do business interests, professional groups and cultural bodies, for example. Unions thus have a "social" role and not just a "business" one.

Second, because unions enable people to act for themselves. Persons are subjects, not objects. They need to represent themselves, not simply be represented by their employer, however benign that employer might be. This is the same principle that good parents follow when they recognize that their children are now adults and so must make their own decisions.

Third, because unions combat the tendency, inherent to market economies, to treat workers as just another market commodity. Good unions not only struggle for decent wages, but also for a legal framework in the workplace, for grievance procedures that guard against arbitrary treatment, for a voice in the operation of the business (since workers are an essential part of the business), and for some measure of economic security.

Fourth, because unions make possible the process of collective bargaining, which is the most successful democratic institution in our society. More than 95% of all collective agreements are reached without resort to a strike or lockout. On any given day, in this country, dozens of collective agreements are being signed without any fuss. Moreover, time lost through strikes is less than 0.5% of all hours worked. This is a small price to pay for a social institution that protects freedom and gives people an effective voice in both their workplace and their society.

Labour unions are human oganizations. They suffer from the failings found in all things human and, like any other human institution, they can sometimes disappoint us. They are also democratic institutions; their decisions reflect both the strengths and the weaknesses of positions based on majority vote. Union activity also tends of its very nature to be very public and visible. There is also the fact that unions sometimes represent a challenge to well-established interests. For all these reasons unions often receive a bad press. So we often need to make a deliberate effort to appreciate unions.

What should this mean in practice for Catholics?

First, it means that we should be supportive of unions, be active in them, and be ready to run for office in them. People are quick to criticize union excesses or mistakes. But unions are like other democratic organizations—they are only as good as their members and their elected officials make them.

Second, it means we should respect legal picket lines. The late Cardinal John O'Connor of New York once remarked: "I unconditionally disapprove … of using facilities where workers are on strike." To "knowingly and deliberately" cross a legitimate picket line, he said, is to express "contempt for collective bargaining."

Sometimes we are slow to practise what we preach. It is, however, encouraging to know that the Vatican's employees are unionized!

Resources for Discussion:

Scripture: *Ecclesiastes* 4: 9-12

Social Documents: *Mater et Magistra*, nos. 97-103; *Laborem Exercens*, no. 20

Questions for Discussion:

- Catholics sometimes protest today: "But unions are pro-abortion!" What are we to think of this claim?

- People sometimes say: "Unions have become too powerful!" What do you think of this claim?

- Why are companies like Wal-Mart and McDonald's so anti-union? How should we feel about patronizing anti-union companies?

Suggested video to end the meeting:

Unions (National Film Board of Canada)

22. The right to strike

From Pope Leo XIII's *Rerum Novarum* in, 1891, to Pope John Paul II's *Centesimus Annus,* in 1991, Catholic social thought has evolved. This evolution, or "development of doctrine" is evident in the Church's teaching on the right to strike.

Pope Leo, though a man of openness and a great pioneer, was also a man of his time. In *Rerum Novarum*, he saw class divisions in society as "natural", he viewed society as an organic whole in which everyone had an assigned place, which called for obedience. Hence, he regarded conflict as "unnatural". For this reason he was distrustful of strike action, and hoped that action by the state would prevent the need for workers to resort to strikes. Pope Pius X and Pope Benedict XV both saw strikes as contributing to "class struggle," and lending support to Marxism. So in general, they opposed the use of the strike. Again though, it is important to remember the world in which they lived. For example, Pius X spoke of social inequality as a "work of God."

Pius XI, in his 1931 document, provides an analysis of capitalism that is radical in some respects . But he also speaks with some admiration of the movement of "corporatism" that was being tried in some European countries. He admired its efforts to bring capital and labour together in a new ordering of society, and in a famous statement that has often been taken out of context he mentions that within that particular system of corporatism "strikes and lockouts are forbidden." (*Quadragesimo Anno*, no. 94). In time, corporatism came to be seen as tending to fascism and totalitarianism. Indeed Pope Pius XI himself began to realize this more clearly as he witnessed the repressive activities of Hitler's Germany and Mussolini's Italy.

Pope John XXIII's 1961 *Mater et Magistra* is the first truly modern social encyclical. In the section beginning at no. 97, he embraces the modern labour union, the institution of collective bargaining, and the right of workers to have an effective voice in all the institutions that affect their lives.

Pope John Paul II's *Laborem Exercens* speaks clearly of labour unions as indispensable elements of social life, as being engaged in a struggle for social justice, a struggle that is described as "normal." It goes on:

"One method used by unions in pursuing the just rights of their members is the strike or work stoppage, as a kind of ultimatum to the competent bodies, especially the employers. This method is recognized by Catholic social teaching as legitimate in the proper conditions and within just limits. In this connection workers should be assured the right to strike, without being subjected to personal penal sanctions for taking part in a strike" (no. 20).

This historical overview emphasizes how present-day Catholic social teaching has come to the view that non-violent conflict is not in itself unnatural, nor necessarily improper. Pope John Paul's words on the subject of conflict resemble the words of a 1980 Working Party Report from the Church of Scotland, which states: "Nor is the fact that conflict is brought out into the open always a bad thing; it can be a sign of health in an organisation. ... The ultimate power of a trade union rests on the right of its members to withdraw their labour. This right is part of every person's birthright in a free society."

The point being made is that labour unions belong in a market economy, where basic decisions result from power in the marketplace. Unions also belong in a democratic society, where workers have the right to an effective voice in the conditions that affect their daily life. To take away the right to strike is to undermine that power and to muzzle that voice. As the U.S. Bishops say in their 1986 *Economic Justice for All*, "Partnerships between labour and management are possible only when both groups possess real freedom and *power* to influence decisions." (no. 302. Emphasis added).

Catholic social teaching today clearly sees unionization and the associated institution of collective bargaining as meaningless without the attendant right to strike.Vatican II calls the strike "a necessary, though ultimate, means for the defence of the workers' own rights and fulfillment of their just desires" (*Constitution on the Church in the Modern World,* no. 68).

Yet, why not insist that the parties talk things out rather than resorting to a strike? Of course they must talk, and that is the whole point of collective bargaining. Moreover, the right to strike ensures that the talking will be serious. But the need to go on strike, in some instances, is a result of the fact that people have vested interests and social loyalties that often stand in the way of their ability to hear one another or to see one another's point of view. It is Catholic teaching that a strike should be avoided wherever possible. For strikes can sometimes harden attitudes and feed feelings of bitterness. Alternatives to strikes should always be considered. However it is imperative that such alternatives should result from the free choice of the parties.

According to recent Catholic social documents, the conditions required for a strike to be just and morally legitimate are:

First, there must be a *just cause*. Sometimes it requires a careful look at a situation before one discovers the actual cause, which may be associated with the very structures of the workplace and the fundamental attitudes of the employer. These need to be addressed, because workers will rebel against them in some way.

Second, the strike must be a *last resort*. Other means of settling the dispute must have failed. This does not mean they must all have been tried. For there are situations in which it is clear to everyone that other means are simply stalling tactics.

Third, there must be a reasonable *hope of success*. Here again, it is not always easy to define success. It may be that the strike brings a long-standing injustice to public attention and sets in motion forces that will address those injustices.

Fourth, the harm done by the strike must be *counterbalanced* by the good to be hoped for. It is important here not to exaggerate the harm done. For example, in many cases, lost business can be regained fairly quickly.

Fifth, the strike must be carried out by just means. In other words those on strike must do all they can to respect the rights of others.

Resources for Discussion:

Scripture: *Micah* 6: 6-8

Social Documents: *Centesimus Annus*, no. 43

Questions for Discussion:

- Do you think strikes cause a lot of harm? If so, how can we justify them?

- Strikes are forbidden in what are called "essential services." Some might say, if we can do without strikes in those situations why can't we do without them in all situations?

- What are some of the alternatives to strikes that the two sides might freely agree to try in some situations?

23. "Contracting out": good business or degradation of work?

In her best-selling book, *No Logo*, published in 2000, Canadian writer, Naomi Klein, presents a disturbing picture of the ultimate form of "contracting out". Huge transnational corporations like Nike no longer do *any manufacturing at all*. They contract out *all* the work, and concentrate simply on promoting their logo (the "swish" in Nike's case). The practice of contracting out, or outsourcing, has literally exported entire industries to Third World sweatshops. (Bluestone and Bennett identified outsourcing as a major factor in the process they called *The Deindustrialization of America* [New York 1982])

Meanwhile, contracting out also continues to be embraced in our own communities by more and more educational and health facilities, different levels of government, as well as various industries and construction companies.

What is "contracting out"? F.J. Young described it, years ago, as "an arrangement with an outside firm entered into by an employer whereby production or service work which was or could have been done by his own employees and equipment is to be performed by the outside firm." Who could quarrel with that? Might it not just be a good business decision taken in the interests of efficiency? If we look at it carefully we will find a practice that in most cases deeply offends some of the most fundamental principles of Catholic social teaching. Think of some concrete examples. A school board no longer hires its own janitors who *belong* to a particular school community, but arranges for an outside cleaning service to drop into different schools at various times and perform particular services. A municipality no longer operates its own bus system but arranges for some large transportation company to provide services to the community. A federal department no longer does its own testing, but contracts this out to the lowest private bidder.

What are the effects of this practice?

First, there is ample evidence that contracting out usually means changing from a unionized to a non-unionized work force. That has been the experience with educational and health facilities and government services here at home, for example, and it is very clear in the transfer of manufacturing operations from Ontario to "right to work" (that is, anti-union) states in the southern U.S., as well as to Mexico and parts of Asia. This flies in the face of Catholic teaching, which speaks, not just of the *right* to unionize but of the *social need* for unions ("an indispensable element of social life," in the words of Pope John Paul II). It also, in the words of Professor Young (quoted above), frustrates public policy, because Canadian law has historically viewed unionization as an important social good.

Second, contracting out also nearly always means a substantial decrease in salary as well as a loss of other benefits and protection for the people performing the work in question. Indeed this is the "business reason" usually offered for engaging in this practice. In many sectors, such as housekeeping services, and transportation, this means that salaries which were barely adequate to stay above the poverty line, even with union contracts, are now well below that level. Of course when we look at entire manufacturing operations being contracted out to sweatshop operators in Latin America, the Philippines, and China, for example, we see pay rates and working conditions that are appalling and totally inhuman. Employers who engage in contracting out create a "distance" between themselves and those who are performing the work they need. There is a "contractor" who stands between them and the employees in question. Yet that "distance" and that intervening "contractor" cannot change the fact that they are *morally responsible* for the low wages or the lack of social benefits that their contract employees must accept. Ultimately these people are working for *them,* and are owed, among other things, a *just* wage, not the "going wage".

Third, anyone who seriously considers the overall impact of outsourcing will see that it is simply a modern way of reducing human labour to a "commodity." Nearly every official document of Catholic social teaching has seen that as something utterly degrading. To grasp this point better, we need to remind ourselves of what human work is meant to be. It is, as Pope John Paul II has shown so vividly, the principal manner in which human beings carry out their role as "the image of God." A person's work is his or her "calling," his or her way of caring for God's world, in God's Name, as God's manager. As such it is meant to contribute to human growth, freedom and sense of purpose in life.

Yet how does contracting out stand in the way of human work being regarded as one's vocation? Ask the workers involved! Here in Ontario, for example, people who worked for a school board, a hospital, a municipality, a government service, were conscious of themselves as part of an established and respected human enterprise, they belonged to the "team" or the "community," sharers in responsibility for that enterprise. This is in keeping with Catholic social teaching that business enterprises need to take on the character of a community of persons in which, as far as possible, all the members of that community have some share in the management of the enterprise. Now these workers are told that they are no longer part of that undertaking or that institution. They are no longer a valued member of the school staff, a responsible representative of the city, a respected part of the health care operation, a proud member of the company that manfactures a socially respected product. Instead they are, literally, "hired hands." Their only importance is to provide some service that is measured in purely economic terms. Some years ago, the head of one of the largest chains of private nursing homes in Ontario frankly admitted that no business operation can expect the same degree of dedication from people who are simply employees of a contractor as one sees in people who are truly part of the operation.

In the words of Pope John Paul II, "work is for the person, not the person for work." The most serious violation of that principle is any situation that treats a person as a mere "instrument of production." Indeed, any situation which considers "human labour solely according to its economic purpose" is really "an error of materialism" because it "directly or indirectly places the personal (human activity, moral values, and such matters) in a position of subordination to material reality" (*Laborem Exercens*, no. 13). Contracting out, whatever the intentions of those who institute it, actually promotes a purely materialistic view of human work. However much it may sometimes look like "good business", it is a practice we should oppose.

Resources for Discussion:

Scripture: *James* 5: 1-6

Social Documents: *Centesimus Annus*, no. 35

Questions for Discussion:

- The need to cut costs is the reason most often given for "contracting out." What are we to think of this?

- The charge is that "contracting out" *de-unionizes* our economy. What about those (fairly rare) situations in which the work is actually contracted out to a unionized employer?

- What instances of "contracting out" do you see in the community? What effects do you see resulting from this practice in those situations?

Suggested video to end the meeting:

Shutdown! (National Film Board of Canada)

24. "Replacement workers"

From time to time, during a legal strike, we read of "replacement workers" being brought in to do the work of the people on strike. Nearly always, this sort of action leads to confrontation and bitterness, and often to violence as well.

In November, 1992, Ontario's NDP government passed legislation banning the use of replacement workers in any situation where there had been a strike vote of more than 60 per cent. One of the first actions of the Conservative government that later came to power in Ontario was to rescind this law. From the standpoint of Catholic social teaching, it is truly unfortunate that "replacement workers" are once again legal in Ontario.

The position of the Canadian Catholic Bishops on this matter is clear. In a letter to the federal Minister of Labour on October 20, 1992, the Social Affairs Commission of the Canadian Conference of Catholic Bishops called for federal legislation to ban the use of replacement workers. It also urged the Minister to call on the various provinces to enforce such legislation in their own territories, if they already have it on their books, or to pass such legislation if they do not. Why did the Bishops take this position? Why is this an issue for Catholic social teaching?

First, our attitude to the use of replacement workers during a legal strike has much to do with the *picture* we have of what a business actually is. Some people speak of the "owner's business" being threatened by a ban on replacement workers. Clearly, such people think (incorrectly) that the owners of the "capital" (the lands, buildings, materials) are by that very fact the owners of the business. Catholic social teaching questions the whole notion of a business being an object of ownership. This is because a business involves not only the owners of capital, and the management personnel, but also all the other workers. Such a community of people cannot be an object of ownership. Moreover, owners of capital do not, through their ownership of *things,* thereby acquire rights over *persons*.

"In economic enterprises it is persons who are joined together, that is, free and independent human beings created to the image of God. Therefore taking account of the prerogatives of each – owners or employers, management or labour – and without doing harm to the necessary unity of management, the active sharing of all in the administration and profits of these enterprises in ways to be properly determined should be promoted." (*Constitution on the Church in the Modern World, no. 68*).

To set aside this picture of a business enterprise as a sort of partnership, in favour of viewing the business as something "owned" by the owners of capital, is to treat the workers as nothing more than "instruments of production". But when we do this, when we treat "human labour solely according to its economic purpose" we are guilt of "an error of materialism" because we "directly or indirectly place the spiritual and the personal (man's activity, moral values, and such matters) in a position of subordination to material reality." (*On Human Work*, no. 13)

In fact not only is the image of a business as an object of ownership morally questionable, it is also increasingly antiquated in today's economy. Authoritarian management simply has no place in today's world. Genuine workplace partnership has to come about, and it is in the best interests of the business to promote such an attitude of partnership. This kind of attitude is bound to make the business not only more human but also more efficient. However the hiring of replacement workers during a strike, and the message it sends to the workers being replaced is the very antithesis of a partnership mentality.

Second, it is important to consider the experience of the one Canadian jurisdiction that has for many years had a law banning the use of replacement workers during strikes. The province of Quebec introduced such a law in 1978, and made some amendments to it in 1983. Since the law was introduced there has been a marked decline in picket line violence in that province, and a significant improvement in the collective bargaining climate there. These changes are generally recognized as resulting at least in part from the law banning replacement workers. We should also note that this law did not bring about a flight of capital from Quebec, nor a noticeable decline in business activity there.

Third, we have to recognize that employees have a long-term stake in the success of the business of which they are a part, and in the continued operation of their collective bargaining process. If they are on a legal strike, and protected by a law banning replacement workers, they are not going to use this situation to bring about lasting harm to the business. It is *their* business too, and it is in their interest to see that it succeeds.

Resources for Discussion:

Scripture: *Sirach* 7: 18-20

Social Documents: *Mater et Magistra*, no. 91

Questions for Discussion:

- What are the effects of "replacement workers" on (1) the permanent employees; (2) the institution of collective bargaining (with its associated right to strike); (3) the public?

- A business is not a "thing" to be owned but a community of people engaged in a common enterprise. What steps might be taken to help people see this?

- How can all the workers in a business have some "share in management"?

25. Restoring a "sabbath" attitude to life

It is only about 25 years since the Ontario legislature debated the question of whether or not municipalities should be given the power to permit businesses to open on Sunday. Today Sunday shopping, and therefore *Sunday work* for the employees affected, is considered normal in most parts of Canada. A further sign of the cultural change that has taken place is the fact that most people now report they have less free time than they had five years ago. A recent poll showed that 81% of white-collar workers are now accepting business calls on their own time, thus letting their job encroach on their home life. We are becoming a society *obsessed* with work, *trapped* in work.

In Catholic social teaching, work has great dignity. It is the ordinary way in which most of us carry out our role as "images of God," managing God's world, caring for God's world, as God intended us to do. However that same Social Teaching reminds us that work is *not* our highest activity. Our ability to work is not as important, for example, as our ability to love, or to know God, or to pray. Medieval educators distinguished between the liberal arts and the servile arts, and there was never any doubt about which were the higher arts. Whereas the servile arts prepare us to do various kinds of work, the liberal arts enable us to seek and appreciate the truth, to love and enjoy the good and the beautiful. Those higher activities are symbolized by the Old Testament practice of observing the *sabbath*.

What Christians and Catholics need, however, is not just a return to better Sunday (sabbath) observance, though that is important. We need above all to take a new *attitude* into daily life. We need to recover, and incorporate into daily life, an approach to the world that leads us to appreciate far more all those realities that do not result from our work: life, the earth, nature, beauty, love, friendship. All these come freely from the hand of God.

Recovering a "sabbath" *attitude*, something that will be part of our daily life and not just a Sunday practice, means facing some of the contemporary tendencies that have distorted our approach to work.

The first tendency is *greed*, both personal and corporate. Since the 17th century, the pursuit of wealth has become not only socially acceptable but even socially desirable. Earlier ages rightly regarded the seeking of wealth for its own sake (rather than seeking only what is needed for a modest lifestyle) as something contemptible and unnatural. To live only by the principle that "time is money" is to sin against God's gift of time.

The second tendency is *our obsession with work*. For many today, work has become a kind of religion, something that takes over their life. The "workaholic" is someone who is truly poor, because he or she is unable to appreciate larger areas of life.

The third, and perhaps most serious, tendency is *pride*. As moderns, we usually act on the assumption that nothing important will happen, nothing helpful will take place, without human effort and human science. In contrast to this outlook we have to learn again to "listen" to God, and to "listen" to God's world, not just try to manipulate them.

A "sabbath" attitude includes at least *four* elements. First, it includes a sense of *freedom*. "Leisure" implies a certain degree of mastery over one's time. However it is not just a freedom *from* other things, like work, but a freedom to be oneself and to do what one considers worthwhile. Second, it involves having a genuine sense of what is *humanly worthwhile*, such as the pursuit of truth for its own sake, the development and enjoyment of one's fundamental human capacities, the appreciation of cultural goods. Third, it includes the ability to *let go* and learn to appreciate what is simply "there" in our world, and to let reality speak to us. Finally, it also involves a spirit of *celebration*, that is, a delight in God and in what we receive from God.

In order to develop an attitude of leisure, there are several *questions* that we should ask ourselves regularly:

What *attitudes* do I bring to my daily life and my daily work?

How do I regard education? Do I see it only as job-related?

What is my relation to nature, to reading, to the arts?

How do I spend my Sunday? Do I avoid Sunday shopping?

How big a part does avarice play in my life?

Resources for Discussion:

Scripture: *Deuteronomy* 5: 12-15; *Mark* 2: 27-28

Social Documents: *Constitution on the Church in the Modern World*, no. 61; *Octogesima Adveniens*, no. 41. *Mater et Magistra*, nos. 245-253.

Questions for Discussion:

Note: Consider either the questions posed at the end of the chapter (above) or the ones that follow:

- A recent survey showed that a sizeable percentage of people in Ontario are not taking all the vacation time to which they are entitled. What do you conclude from this?

- Why did earlier ages regard the seeking of wealth for its own sake as "unnatural"?

- Is "leisure" the same thing as "recreation"?

26. Farming

The U.S. ban on Prince Edward Island potatoes, lasting from the fall of 2000 until the spring of 2001, cost the farmers of that province many millions of dollars. The fact that the very livelihood of so many people could be put in jeopardy by the unilateral, and largely unjustified, decision of a powerful foreign government, shows how vulnerable our Canadian farmers are. Yet, though they make up only 2% of our population, those farmers are responsible for nothing less than our Canadian food security.

Catholic social teaching calls on us to support our farmers, wholeheartedly and intelligently. Over the past 50 years there has been a growing body of official Catholic statements on agriculture. Partly, this has been the result of an increasing awareness of the esteem in which the Bible holds the farmer. Partly, it has been because we have seen persistent hunger and malnutrition in our world, in spite of bountiful crops, and the popes have asked what is wrong with our food system that such a thing could happen.

Six principles have become prominent in modern Catholic social teaching on agriculture.

The Nobility of Farming - In 1974, Pope Paul VI, talking about agriculture, said that what was needed above all was a radical change of attitude toward farming. For our world attaches little importance to farmers, while making heroes of people in much less crucial occupations. "Farmers," he said, "must esteem and be faithful to the way of life they have chosen." Pope John Paul II called people to hold the *vocation* of farming in the highest regard. "The world of agriculture, which provides society with the goods it needs for its daily sustenance, is of fundamental importance." (*On Human Work,* no. 21)

The Responsibility Associated with Farmland - Only 11% of Canada is suitable for farming, and only 1% of it is Class I farmland (much of that concentrated in southern Ontario). Our attitude to this precious resource must be one of *stewardship*. We are "aliens and tenants*"* in the land (*Lev. 25:23)*, and God is the owner.

The Importance of the family farm - This ideal of maintaining and supporting the family farm was especially promoted by Pope John XXIII, who grew up on a farm. While it is increasingly difficult to say just what constitutes a "family farm" in today's economy, we can at least understand what the popes are saying when they point to the human values that are promoted when farming is in the hands of a *community of persons* rather than an impersonal business enterprise.

The Need for Grass Roots Participation - It is extremely dangerous to permit the production of food to be concentrated in a few hands (as happens when large agribusiness concerns take over whole sectors of agriculture). Farmers themselves must be genuinely involved in decision-making regarding this vital activity.

The Value of Self-Reliance - There is a great need to promote a world-wide policy of *self-reliance* in the production of food. The emphasis, in any area of the world, should be first and foremost on producing food for that region, with the surplus being available for export. This principle clearly opposes the widespread practice of producing food primarily for export, a practice that is largely responsible for the inability of many poor countries to feed themselves. The Catholic Church has called for wide distribution of land ownership and tighter control of market forces in agriculture.

The Importance of Using Appropriate Technology - This issue was addressed by Pope John Paul II in especially strong terms in his January 1, 1990 Address for the World Day of Peace. He pointed to the harm done by certain herbicides, by the reckless exploitation of land and water, and by indiscriminate genetic manipulation.

What can be done here in Canada? Farmers themselves should avoid simply buying into the marketplace mentality. They must do all they can to build up a sense of solidarity within the farming community. Co-operative ventures of various kinds are also still important for them. Above all though, everyone, farmers and non-farmers alike, looking at present trends in agriculture, must be much more aware of how much is at stake: food safety, food security, self-reliance. We must be ready to support our farmers politically, economically and socially, realizing that the dominant food system has to be radically reformed. Meanwhile it is also important that Canadian residents support local farmers by making the deliberate decision to buy local produce at every opportunity.

Resources for Discussion:

Scripture: *Leviticus* 25: 23-4; *Luke* 12: 16-21

Social Documents: *Mater et Magistra*, nos. 144-149; *Laborem Exercens*, no. 21

Questions for Discussion:

- "The dominant food system has to be radically reformed". In what ways?

- Are the free trade agreements good or bad for our farming communities?

- What attitude should we adopt toward genetically-modified crops?

Suggested video to end the meeting:

Cradled by the Hand of God (National Catholic Rural Life Conference)

27. Is the social welfare state dead?

In 1989, the communist regimes of Eastern Europe, often referred to as socialist economies, collapsed. Two years later, when Pope John Paul II published *Centesimus Annus,* a social document commemorating the 100th anniversary of official Catholic social teaching, he used the occasion to rejoice in the demise of those socialist regimes, and to do some dancing on Marx's grave. Some have interpreted this 1991 document as an endorsement of liberal capitalism, and so have celebrated the end of "the welfare state," which they regard as "socialist." Such people have not read *Centesimus Annus* very carefully, nor have they reflected sufficiently on some of the underlying principles of Catholic social teaching.

Pope John Paul was well-informed on economic issues. When he was preparing *Centesimus Annus* he actually met with an international group of fifteen economists, including a Nobel laureate, and sought their advice. He accepted the realities of today's economy. He recognized the fact that the capitalist, market principle appears to be the most efficient instrument for organizing a modern economy, and acknowledged the freedom that it appears to provide for people. He saw too the sort of incentive it provides for entrepreneurs, and he praised those who use their ingenuity to create wealth. He makes it clear, however, that the Church does not unequivocally endorse liberal capitalism. He points out that "the Church has no models to present . . . [instead] the Church offers her social teaching" (see *Centesimus Annus,* sections 42 and 43), In making this statement he is taking the long-held position that the Church endorses no particular ideology, either capitalist or socialist. Its concern is for whatever will respect and enhance the dignity of the human person.

Here it is helpful to return to Pope John XXIII's great document, *Mater et Magistra.* There, we find expressed the basic principle that, for an economy to be just, it must not only produce an abundance of needed goods and services, and it must not only distribute those goods and services equitably, but *it must also make the producers themselves more human in the process* (no. 83).

If the economy is for the sake of persons, and not persons for the sake of the economy, we must ask, What kind of *person* is a particular society and economy creating? Is it creating a person who is conscious of what human dignity entails? Is it favouring authentic human development? Is it providing the opportunities for each person to develop a sense of responsibility, and to exercise personal initiative and creativity?

A particularly intriguing passage in *Centesimus Annus* states that a just economy requires that any *business* should be seen as a "society of persons" (no. 43). It is fascinating to reflect on what that would involve if businesses really followed it!

We can now look at section 48 of *Centesimus Annus* (a section about which there is considerable debate), in which Pope John Paul II speaks about the social welfare state. There he says that such states sometimes violate the principle of subsidiarity by putting into the hands of public (government) agencies matters that could be handled privately.

"By intervening directly and depriving society of its responsibility, the Social Assistance State leads to a loss of human energies and an inordinate increase of public agencies, which are dominated more by bureaucratic ways of thinking than by concern for serving their clients, and which are accompanied by an enormous increase in spending. In fact it would appear that needs are best understood and satisfied by people who are closest to them and who act as neighbours to those in need. It should be added that certain kinds of demands often call for a response which is not simply material but which is capable of perceiving the deeper human need. One thinks of the condition of refugees, immigrants, the elderly, the sick, and all those circumstances which call for assistance, such as drug abusers: all these people can be helped effectively only by those who offer them genuine fraternal support, in addition to the necessary care."

We recognize at once the truth of what is being said here. There is simply no substitute for the great works of charity. Many enlightened government policies reflect an awareness of this truth, for example the federal government's Joint Assistance Program for sponsoring refugees, in which government assumes financial responsibility for the refugees for a two-year period as long as an approved sponsoring group, usually a church, provides all the needed human assistance.

Some people have appealed to Pope John Paul's remarks as support for their goal of "getting government out of the economy", privatizing public services, cutting back on social programs, and "reducing welfare rolls." But in talks he gave during the weeks surrounding the appearance of *Centesimus Annus* the pope made it clear that he was not condemning social welfare programs as such, but rather "systematic welfarism", which violates human dignity with programs that actually stand in the way of people taking responsibility for themselves wherever possible. This is in line with what he says in section 32 of this document when he points out that economic development today depends not so much on land or capital as on persons possessing technical skills and know-how. When people possess such skills, they are more able to act on their own initiative, and to stand on their own feet, without being overly-dependent on the state. The pope's vision, then, is one of an economy in which social and economic forces actively contribute to people growing in the exercise of personal initiative, freedom and responsibility.

This picture is also promoted by Pope John XXIII where he says that balance is needed between personal initiative and state intervention in the economy. After pointing to the dangers that Pope John Paul would later mention, however, he also adds: "Where, on the other hand, the good offices of the State are lacking or deficient, incurable disorder ensues; in particular, the unscrupulous exploitation of the weak by the strong" (*Mater et Magistra,* number 58).

Clearly, Pope John Paul offers no comfort to those who would cut back so much on social programs and social welfare benefits as to compromise the well-being and personal development of those persons who truly require them. He writes in section 10: "the more that individuals are defenceless within a given society, the more they require the care and concern of others, *and in particular the intervention of governmental authority"* (italics added). He states that he is here defending a principle that appears in the very encyclical whose anniversary he is celebrating, *Rerum Novarum*, where Pope Leo XIII makes the statement, "The richer class have many ways of shielding themselves, and stand less in need of help from the State, whereas the mass of the poor have no resources of their own to fall back upon, and must chiefly depend upon the assistance of the State." (no. 29). In today's society, even in prosperous countries like our own, there are many such persons, and in fact far more than can be helped by voluntary agencies alone. Vatican II's *Constitution on the Church in the Modern World* asserts that "The complex circumstances of our day make it necessary for public authority to intervene *more often* in social, economic and cultural matters in order to bring about favourable conditions which will give more effective help to citizens and groups in their free pursuit of man's total well-being." (No. 75. Italics added. cf. also *Mater et Magistra*, no. 54).

What has been called "the welfare state" may indeed no longer be viable. However this does not justify the dismantling or downsizing of needed social programs, particularly where the motive is primarily to satisfy the appetite for tax cuts, which mainly benefit the rich. Catholic social teaching, with its commitment, not only to the principle of subsidiarity but also to that of solidarity, will always insist on the need for an array of publicly-financed universal social programs, and for a compassionate and responsible involvement of the government in the economy.

Resources for Discussion:

Scripture: *1 Cor* 12: 14-26

Social Documents: *Constitution on the Church in the Modern World*, no. 63.

Questions for Discussion:

- What features of our Canadian society make us, in some ways, a "social welfare state"?

- What sort of *new* universal social programs do you think we need in Canada?

- What do you think of the universal social programs we presently have in this country?

28. Politics

Scarcely a day goes by when the news media do not make critical comments about some politician. In one sense, this is legitimate; political figures must be accountable to the people they represent. In another sense though, such criticism tends to foster a spirit of cynicism towards politics in general, and this is unfortunate. Pope Pius XI once wrote: "Politics has to do with the interests of the whole of society; from this angle, it is the domain of charity in its largest sense, of political charity, of the charity of the City." What he meant was that a willingness to serve people in public office is an especially noble form of love for others.

The first thing Catholics should do is to help set a tone of high regard for political office and of genuine respect for those people who are willing to serve in politics. In a 1998 talk, Pope John Paul II spoke out against exaggerated attacks on political leaders and institutions, and he added: "Neither those accusations nor the rather widespread opinion according to which politics is an occupation fraught with moral danger, in the least justifies the abstention of Christians from public life."

A second thing Catholics can do is to make sure we do not ask either too much or too little of politics. In *Quadragesimo Anno*, Pope Pius XI laid down this principle: for social progress, *two* things are needed, the reform of *persons*, and the reform of *social institutions*. People on the far left of the political spectrum often speak as if all our human ills could be corrected if we just had the right kind of laws, and the appropriate social and economic institutions. People on the far right tend to speak as if all our troubles could be dealt with if we just had good people.

Catholic social teaching moves down the middle in this debate. On the one hand, we need *personal conversion*. There is no substitute for the effort to become, with God's grace, good persons. This in fact is the most important thing each of us can do for the common good. That personal goodness will, in turn, lead us to reach out in loving care to those in need, and to involve ourselves in voluntary service to the community. We must also remember the wise words of St. Thomas Aquinas, that there are serious limitations to what can be achieved through law-making, and that man-made laws cannot prohibit all that is prohibited by natural law. (I-IIae, 96, art. 2, 3). On the other hand, we must recognize that much of what we owe one another as humans can only be accomplished by passing *good laws* and establishing appropriate *social institutions*. In this sense, personal charity can never take the place of what is owed to others in justice.

Third, Catholics should follow certain principles when judging candidates and political parties. In their statements, *Choosing a Government* and *Taking Stock,* the Catholic Bishops of Ontario list eleven such principles. They include: the dignity of every human person, the common good, equitable treatment, stewardship of the environment, a balanced approach to private property, the right of all to gainful employment, the rights of workers, the rights of the marginalized, the sacredness of human life at all stages, and the principles of solidarity and subsidiarity.

Finally, Catholics should realize that politics is the *art of the possible*. So we need to have reasonable expectations in politics. Look for the best people we can find among those on offer. Accept the principle of the lesser evil. Don't abstain from voting or from participating in the political process just because you can't get the person or the exact policy you would like to have.

Moreover, we must keep in mind that the people we elect are not just *delegates*. They are not just machines to reflect the views of their party or the electors. They are *persons* who must take their own stands based on personal convictions, including their religious convictions. The well-known Catholic politician, Claude Ryan, said, "in order to be effective in politics, one must first be a good politician, i.e. a politician who strives to be competent, close to the people, dedicated, productive, knowledgeable, honest, truthful, and electable. A person who wants to succeed in politics must first establish his or her presence at that level, which is that of the moral virtues."

100

So when deciding how to vote, we need to look at the candidate's character and integrity, experience, and general approach to public life. We should give special emphasis to his or her stand on life issues, but not ordinarily be single issue voters.

"A general election must never be confused with a single-issue referendum", say the Bishops of England and Wales in their 1996 document, *The Common Good and the Catholic Church's Social Teaching* (no. 65). So we must consider *all* aspects of an election, including who has a genuine chance of winning, and then do the best we can.

Resources for Discussion:

Scripture: *Romans* 13: 1-7

Social Documents: *Constitution on the Church in the Modern World*, no. 75

Questions for Discussion:

- Why are so many people today cynical about politics and politicians? Is such cynicism justified?

- Can good laws change people for the better over the course of time?

- What do you think of the movement for governments to hold referendums on important issues?

Suggested videos to end the meeting:

Faithful Citizenship (United States Catholic Conference)

Political Responsibility (United States Catholic Conference)

29. Working for social change

Walking a picket line, participating in a boycott, lobbying our politicians, taking part in a protest, these are all activities that many Catholics find distasteful and contrary to their understanding of the gospel. After all, they say, aren't we committed to forgiveness, reconciliation and peace?

Yet. not only are such "disruptive" activities legitimate; they can at times be our moral obligation.

Why should this be so? It is because, for this world to become more human and more just, and so for us to fulfill the Lord's command to love our neighbour, two kinds of conversion are needed, personal and social. The *radical socialist* neglects the need for personal conversion, believing that it is sufficient to change laws and social practices. The *religious individualist* neglects the need for social conversion, believing it is sufficient to change individual hearts. The balanced Christian, who is in touch with the social teaching of the Church, sees the need for both. The season of Lent, for example, regularly calls us to *personal* conversion. However, changing conditions in our society regularly call us to *social* conversion: laws written for an earlier time require replacement; rights not appreciated half a century ago now require recognition and protection; prejudice or unfair practices embedded in our social life require elimination.

How is social change to be brought about? Normally it is accomplished by some form of collective action. But why *action*? Can't we just sit down and talk reasonably with one another?

In social matters, talk alone is often insufficient. This is because all of us tend to get locked into prevailing social attitudes that stand in the way of our seeing things objectively. We tend to identify with the views of our social or economic class. We also, more often than we care to admit, have some vested interest in keeping things the way they are. Often it is only some sort of concerted social action, like a demonstration, a picket line or a boycott that shakes us up enough so we can begin looking at things in a new way.

Yet what about our Lord's words in *Matthew 5:39-41*: "But I say to you, do not resist an evildoer. But if anyone strikes you on the right cheek, turn the other also; and if anyone wants to sue you and take your coat, give your cloak as well; and if anyone forces you to go one mile, go also the second mile." Don't these words forbid us to engage in confrontation? No. These words concern the *attitude* a disciple of Christ should adopt in one-to-one relationships. They call on a disciple who is wronged to adopt a positive, creative attitude to the wrongdoer, rather than a vengeful one. Indeed a spirit of revenge is always wrong, no matter what the situation. But these words are not a directive for social and political action. If we want our Lord's guidance on how to deal with those sorts of action then we should look to passages like the following:

Matthew 10:34: "Do not think that I have come to bring peace to the earth; I have not come to bring peace, but a sword." Jesus is making the point that faithful disciples will provoke opposition and persecution by what they say and by the stands they take.

Mark 11:15-19, where Jesus cleansed the Temple, driving out those who were selling and buying there.

Luke 11:37-54, where Jesus confronted the Pharisees and lawyers regarding their social practices, and did so in such fierce words that we are told they became "very hostile toward him." Similarly, needed social change will often require us to use methods of confrontation and non-violent conflict.

The Second Vatican Council supported such a way of acting when it said: "We cannot refrain from praising those who, renouncing violent action in the vindication of rights, have recourse to means of defence which are otherwise available to weaker parties as well, so long as this is accomplished without violating the rights and obligations of others or of the community." (*Constitution on the Church in the Modern World,* no. 78). Recall also Pope

John Paul II's use of the word "struggle" in his encyclical, *On Human Work.* He said that unions "struggle for social equity, … for the just good. It is not, however, "a fight against others." "Even if in controversial questions it takes on the nature of a struggle against others, this is for the sake of the good of social justice, and not for the sake of 'struggle' itself, nor to destroy the adversary." (no. 20).

There are many situations in which failing to take sides, and deciding simply to remain passive or silent, amounts to condoning social evil. These are, for example, situations in which one side is clearly right and other side clearly wrong, or one side is inflicting injustice and the other side is suffering it. Many white Christians in South Africa, during the period of apartheid, eventually had to come to terms with this fact, and join the movements of peaceful resistance to government policy. We need to ask ourselves regularly if we are hiding behind a false understanding of "peace" in order to avoid confronting social evils in our own society. Peace, after all, is not just the absence of war. It is the fruit of justice and love.

Resources for Discussion:

Scripture: *Revelation* 21: 1-7 & 22-27.

Social Documents: *Octogesima Adveniens*, no. 48

Questions for Discussion:

- We must be ready to engage in "struggle" for social justice, but not to do so just "for the sake of struggle". What might lead people to this latter way of acting?

- What forms of "struggle" taking place in our society at present should we consider supporting to the best of our ability?

- Can you think of any situations in our community or region that need to be addressed by a movement for social change?

Suggested video to end the meeting:

Saul Alinsky Went to War (National Film Board of Canada)

Conclusion: Putting the social teaching of the Church into practice

A man was visiting the Holy Land. In Jerusalem he noticed an elderly Jewish gentleman who spent a long time praying at the Wailing Wall. As the man left the wall, the visitor went up to him, and asked: "How often do you come here to pray?" The man said "Every day. I come here faithfully every day to pray." The visitor was impressed and asked: "What do you pray for?" The old gentleman said: "I pray for peace, peace for the world, peace for Jerusalem." The visitor said: "That's wonderful! Are your prayers answered?" The old gentleman scowled and said: "No they're not. I might as well be talking to a stone wall."

This story might reflect the attitude of many of us who try to put our Church's social teachings into practice. Nonetheless, there are effective actions we can take to apply this teaching in our community and in our world. We do need a lot of patience: we must be prepared to lose many battles; but we will win some too. Consider the following suggestions.

First, we need to *cultivate a proper understanding of lay ministry*. There is an organization in Chicago called the National Center for the Laity. It has been around for over 25 years and publishes a newsletter entitled *Initiatives*. Its favourite theme is that lay ministry is not primarily a matter of doing special things in church, like being a lector, a eucharistic minister, a catechist, and so on. It's not about becoming quasi-clerics. Lay ministry is about applying our faith to our work in daily life. The *Decree on the Laity* of Vatican II makes a similar point quite clearly.

In an exploration of the concept of laity, the theologian Karl Rahner points out that the word "laity" comes from an archaic Greek word, *laos*, whereas the ordinary Greek word for people is *ethnos*. And, when referring

106

to God's people, the Bible uses *laos*, to show that it is talking about a special people, with a special mission in the world. "Laity" are God's People, God's consecrated, priestly people", called and anointed to serve and transform our world.

Thus, Catholics need to be aware of their special mission to let the Gospel shine on their work, to bring to their daily work a new sense of its value and importance. What does it mean to be a Catholic who is a truck driver, a lawyer, a production line worker, a nurse, a teacher?

The sense of Christian vocation can transform a person's approach to daily work, and can lead them to have a great impact on their work environment. We need to see the front line of Christian social action in our activity at our work, and in our involvement with work-related organizations such as our labour union or professional organization. If we realize that we have a mission to transform the world, and make it a better place, then we will be active in these organizations and even ready to run for office in them.

Second, we need to *know the Church's social teaching*. In 1986, the U.S. Bishops published a pastoral letter on the economy, *Economic Justice for All*. They spent years consulting people and working on this wonderful document. But it was severely criticized by a couple of prominent Catholics. In response to them, a letter from a professor of political science at the University of Chicago, who identified himself as a Catholic layman, appeared in the *New York Times* on December 14th, 1986. Among other things, it said the following: "In my parish and in my travels around the country I encounter many Catholics who are proud of the leadership on social and economic policy that the bishops have shown when both national parties have decided that the poor and minorities are out of style and that upscale suburbanites don't want to hear about any more problems … The Pope and the bishops, if you read their words carefully, are raising issues that challenge the positions of the vast majority of political leaders…"

In the social documents of the universal church, and in the social documents of our bishops, here in Canada, and in the United States, we have a treasure. So it is important to be familiar with them. When they become part of us, then things happen in our daily life. Quite spontaneously we begin to raise questions, and to follow certain courses of action. We begin to act in new ways.

Third, we must *learn to do good social analysis*. If we become critical thinkers we will start to question many things in our daily life, as well as in what we read or see on television. It is a matter of cultivating the practice of "see-judge-act".

One helpful resource is the book *Getting Started on Social Analysis,* by Michael Czerny and Jamie Swift. There are also some insightful radio and television programs, and videos.

Fourth, we should *examine our lifestyle*. The way we live affects our openness to appropriate social action, and also preaches a message, one way or another, to others. For one thing, with whom do we spend our time? The "option for the poor" that we read about in social documents seems to suggest that we ought to be at home with the poor, or at least with the 'poorer' in our society. The poor are good for us. Consider also how we use our money. Do we consider the social impact of all our spending and investing? Do we put the real needs of others ahead of our wants? How much do we give to the poor? What kind of vacations do we take? How much do we spend on entertainment, on clothing, on transportation? Finally, are we really ready to take sides, to make choices, and to be prophetic, no matter the personal cost?

Fifth, *know our allies*. When we are concerned about some social issue, we don't usually need to act alone. Often, we will find others in our community who share our concern. We should look at campaigns already being led by our own Canadian Catholic Organization for Development and Peace. Often we will find organized labour involved in the issue in question. There might be some local, provincial or national organization calling attention to a campaign. In particular there are several ecumenical groups committed to important areas of social action. In Ontario, for example, there is ISARC, which is such an important advocate for the poor, and nationally there is KAIROS. There are also ecumenical groups working for a new approach to crime and punishment, and groups that work with aboriginal peoples.

Years ago I served on a local committee associated with the national boycott of the major banks when they were participating in loans to the apartheid government of South Africa. One day, while I was in Toronto for a meeting, I looked up at those big buildings and realized that the biggest of them were the headquarters of the major Canadian banks. I thought, "Good heavens, what can we do against them?" Yet, we won that battle. When Nelson Mandela visited Canada after his release from prison, he thanked the Canadian churches for their role in organizing a boycott that brought the banks to their knees and cut off needed funds from an iniquitous regime. Many of us also remember the United Farm Workers boycott of grapes and lettuce. When Cesar Chavez visited London in the early 1990s he went out of his way to say how much our efforts had helped to bring justice to the farmworkers through new union contracts and through new legislation. Many people today believe that their combined efforts as part of the Jubilee Campaign for forgiveness of debt in the world's poorest countries have begun to have some impact on governments and multilateral institutions.

Sixth, *know something about tactics*. For example here is a tried and true approach in terms of how to deal with adversaries on a social issue. (a) Begin by gathering all the information you can, and discussing it thoroughly together. (b) Then seek dialogue with the target group. (c) If this fails, then engage in publicity; let the public know the issues and try to win public support. (d) If this fails to bring results, then engage in forms of protest. Such protest begins with actions within the accepted rules of behaviour, such as court action, appeal to politicians, etc. Then if this fails, engage in protest that breaks social convention but not the law. This includes such things as boycotts, rent strikes, vigils. Finally, as a last resort, consideration might be given to engaging in controlled civil disobedience.

We should also study the tactics of some of the great leaders of social change, like Saul Alinsky. The NFB film about his movement is still available and very instructive. He perfected the techniques of "cutting an issue", "freezing a target", "building determination to win." Though one may disagree with some of his ideas he is still the pioneer in many of today's non-violent means of social change. When Alinsky died in 1972, Ed Chambers took over as head of his organization, the Industrial Areas Foundation. Chambers, who had long been Alinsky's deputy, is an active Catholic, associated with Chicago's National Centre for the Laity. His new book, *Roots for Radicals* (N.Y. 2004), subtitled "Organizing for Power, Action, and Justice," is a very helpful resource for people engaged in social change.

There are other situations in which what we need is a "community development approach." As Desmond Connor showed years ago, this requires taking the following steps in order: (1) understanding the community in question (its history, values, resources, power bases, etc.); (2) diagnosing the community's problems, but being prepared, as a first project, to deal with a problem that represents a *felt need*, and that can be dealt with successfully; (3) choosing a strategy for development, particularly looking for something about the community that you can build on (its history, its unique resources, etc.); (4) stimulating development, by raising people's level of awareness so that they themselves will ask for more information.

Seventh, *examine our prayer*. It's important to ask ourselves what we pray about. Social efforts we are working on, or engaging in, must be something that we can bring before God and talk over with God readily and confidently. Is this where God wants us? If so, then ask God for courage and push ahead, no matter what the obstacles.